Demonic Dolls

True Tales of Terrible Toys

John Harker

Demonic Dolls: True Tales of Terrible Toys

Copyright © 2015 John Harker

ISBN-13: 978-1514823774

ISBN-10: 1514823772

Photo Credits:

Acknowledgements

I wish to thank the following people for their contributions to my inspiration and knowledge and other help in creating this book: John Ryther, David Sloan, Jayne Harris, Jill Phillips-Lingen, Tim Weisberg, John Zaffis, Fr. Gary Thomas, Fr. Mike Driscoll, the Quesnel Museum of British Columbia, and, of course, Robert.

Some names, locations, and similar identifying details have been changed to protect the identities of the individuals who were either witnesses to or victims of these phenomena.

Table of Contents

Introduction

Who among us hasn't had an encounter with a creepy doll? Perhaps there was one in your own collection as a child that just didn't "fit in." It always seemed to be watching you. It made you feel weird. It was the one you avoided playing with. Maybe your sister had a Baby Alive doll that was just a little bit *too* alive for your comfort zone. Or maybe you remember your brother's G.I. Joe smiling at you once, and everyone knows G.I. Joe never smiles.

Even as adults, many of us continue to have this irrational anxiety around playthings that other people deem cute and cuddly. *Oh, c'mon*, your friends will say. *It's just a doll!* You smile and nod, silently thinking, *yeah, but . . .* Have we seen too many Chucky movies? Or is there an element of truth behind our primitive fears?

Actually, there are many reasons to believe that our primitive ancestors did contribute to our darker perceptions of dolls. After all, dolls have been around since ancient times when belief in magic, monsters, and all things supernatural and preternatural was the norm. Roman girls, after they were too "grown up" to play with toys, dedicated their wooden dolls to goddesses. Sometimes these dolls were then used in magical rituals connected to that particular goddess. In ancient Egypt, priests and magicians used poppets (small effigies of human beings) in ceremonies intended to rid the body of evil or to place curses on those who defied the will of the gods. Early Germanic and Scandinavian tribes were known to use poppets in their various ceremonies. The tradition continued through the ages and was an essential part of European paganism and witchcraft. Records from the Salem witch trials, which cite the use of poppets, show the eventual transference of these practices to the New World.

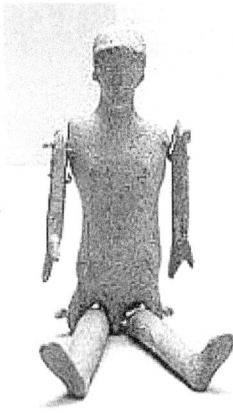

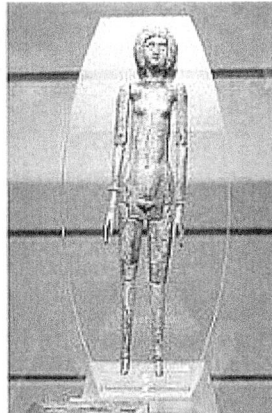

(L) Greek doll, 400-500 BC   (R) Roman doll, 200-300 CE

Of course, when many people think of evil dolls, they think of voodoo dolls. The modern voodoo doll is actually a New World creation, resulting from the mix of West African voodoo (vodun) practices brought over by slaves and European traditions involving poppets. African voodoo used effigies called *bocio* that were designed to be mediators to the spirit world. The belief was that through the bocio, contact could be made with ancestors and deities in order to obtain help, protection, and other needs. The doll itself was not the source of power, merely the vessel through which communication and change took place. Eventually the two traditions, African and European, merged into what is now recognized as the voodoo commonly practiced in places such as Louisiana and Haiti. From that mix came varying types of poppet-style dolls used in rituals to affect both good and bad results.

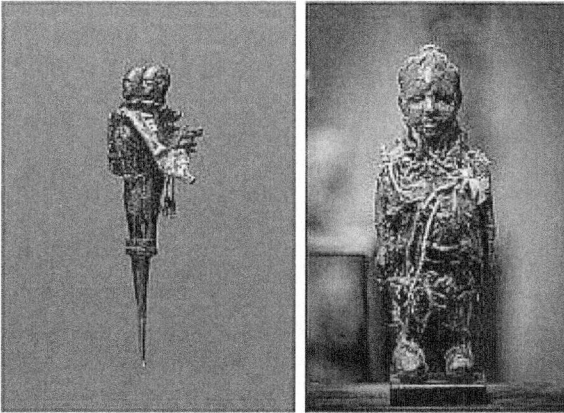

Examples of bocio

While many practitioners of voodoo and other mystical arts utilize dolls in their rituals for positive reasons, like bringing about love, health, and prosperity, there are ill-intentioned individuals who use them for malevolent purposes. Father Gabriele Amorth, Rome's former chief exorcist, explains that objects such as dolls, clothes, photographs, and other personal possessions of an intended target can be "hexed," thereby indirectly imposing a spell on the person the object belongs to. And yes, in some cases, pins are thrust into dolls to cause the victim to experience headaches, stomachaches, and other maladies. The good news is that not just anyone can curse a doll or other object. It takes considerable skill and commitment. "Many sorcerers are inexperienced or unable to follow through; others are simply swindlers," says Fr. Amorth.

If we take Fr. Amorth at his word and accept that there is a dearth of competent hexers out there, you wouldn't think that reports of weird or frightening doll behavior would be all that common. Yet the reports are numerous and are keeping paranormal investigators, clergy members, psychics, mediums, and other such specialists busier than ever. They can't all be cursed, so what else accounts for these hauntings?

The overwhelming consensus among paranormal professionals is that these dolls are affected by spirit energy. The energy could be residual, that is, generated and impressed upon an object from a previous owner. Or it could be a human spirit that has attached itself to the doll, either because the doll belonged to it in life, or simply because it's attracted to it for its physical appearance, just like we are drawn to some things and not others. It could also be an inhuman spirit that has taken up residence in the doll either on its own or because it has been "bound" to it via ritual magic.

Paranormal investigator and author Jayne Harris draws this comparison between haunted houses and haunted objects: "Put in simple terms, if a building can hold residual or intelligent spiritual energy, then it makes sense for other objects to do the same."

If we accept the possibility of haunted houses, or ghosts/spirits in general, it certainly makes sense that they—spirits—could take up residence in a Chatty Cathy or Ballerina Barbie. Father Gary Thomas, the exorcist portrayed in the movie *The Rite*, says: "If a doll or other object had some emotional attachment to a deceased person, I cannot see why it is not possible for a human spirit to attach itself to the object."

And what about an *inhuman* spirit? Is it possible for demons, imps, Djinns, and the like to possess a doll or other object? Fr. Thomas says yes, especially in certain circumstances: "A spirit or a demon can possess an object including a doll. If the doll was used for some kind of rite or ritual that was for occult purposes or Satanic purposes, the object could become possessed."

Father Mike Driscoll, author of the book *Demons, Deliverance, Discernment*, takes a more technical stance on the words used to describe demonic activities: "Only people become possessed. When a demon is attached to or controlling a particular place, an object, or even animals, it is called infestation."

Attachment, possession, infestation—no matter what it's called, it still begs the question, why are dolls such a popular vessel of inhabitation for spirits as opposed to, say, an old bathrobe? Well, first of all, robes *can* become spirit attached. Just ask John Zaffis, demonologist and owner/operator of the Paranormal Museum in Stratford, Connecticut. While it's not a bathrobe per se, a century-old ritual robe hangs in Zaffis' museum along with other articles of clothing such as a wedding dress, a cadet's uniform, a pair of boots, and several hats. These were all things Zaffis removed from people's homes because they were the source of a paranormal disturbance. But by far, the largest number of objects Zaffis has accumulated over the years are dolls. Which brings us back to the question: Why dolls?

Zaffis believes it's because dolls are like miniature people, and as such they are more relatable and attractive to us, especially children, who animate them with energy when they play with them, talk to them, and use their imagination to give them personalities. That energy can "stick" to the doll well after the child is grown. It may remain dormant for years and then become "re-energized" when placed in the right setting.

Not all spirit energy is this residual type, however. There are other, intelligent, spirits that purposely attach themselves to dolls and other objects simply because they are attracted to them. Charles Gotski, paranormal investigator and contributing writer to *Paranormal Underground Magazine*, puts himself in a spirit's shoes when he writes: ". . . if I were deceased, I might want to be attached to something that kind of resembled what I remember my human form to look like, at least to some extent." His take on why dolls are such popular targets for spirit attachment is simple: "A doll represents a way to stay connected to a world that the spirit was once a part of."

As quaint as it might sound for a spirit to want to hang around for nostalgic reasons, it's really not in the best interest of those of us still living. Depending on the nature of the spirit—be it benign, mean, mischievous, or outright evil—the activity it causes can be extremely upsetting to humans. Spirit energy feeds off of our human emotions, so the more fear a person exhibits and feels when, say, a doll blinks at them, the stronger that spirit will become and the more it will escalate its activities. Maybe next time the doll will move across the room.

So what should you do if you suspect you've got a haunted doll on your hands? First, don't panic. No matter how many times you've seen that '70s made-for-TV-movie featuring Karen Black being chased around her apartment by a knife-wielding Zuni fetish doll, that's not likely to happen to you. You may have a problem with a pesky spirit, or even a worst-case scenario of a demon-infested doll, but there is always help available. Contact your spiritual advisor. Reach out to a reputable paranormal investigator. Remain positive. For religious people, this means pray and ask for protection and help. Don't attempt your own "exorcism," as this could just make things worse, sort of like swatting at wasps and making them angrier. Seek the help of a professional if you think you need this sort of action. You can also try disposing of the doll. Burying it or weighing it down and tossing it in deep or running water can often remedy the situation.

Hopefully you've chosen this book not because you're dealing with your own haunted doll situation, but because you are interested in reading about *other people's* haunted dolls. To that end, I enjoin you to continue on—with an open mind and an inquisitive nature—as I begin by introducing you to perhaps the most famous haunted doll in the world . . . Robert.

Chapter 1

Robert

"I was skeptical the first time I met Robert, but he wasted no time making me a believer."

– David Sloan, author and paranormal investigator

In the late 1890s, Dr. Thomas Otto, a prominent physician and businessman in Key West, Florida, commissioned the building of a large, upscale house to accommodate his growing family. Decades later, this Victorian-era residence at 534 Eaton Street would become known as the Artist's House, a reflection of the eventual livelihood and passion of the youngest Otto, Robert Eugene, or Gene, as he was normally called.

Family journals indicate that Gene was painting before he could even talk. The family owned two drug stores on the island, which sold a variety of art supplies in addition to other wares, and which was probably the source of young Gene's early encounters with paints and brushes. As much as art enthralled Gene, there was another presence in his life that captivated him even more, and one which would go on to become a legend in its own right. Its name was Robert.

Robert was Gene's doll. It stood about three feet tall and was usually seen dressed in a sailor's uniform. It was stuffed with fine wood shavings, covered with felt, and featured shoe buttons for eyes. The common legend surrounding Robert's origins goes something like this:

Gene had a Bahamian nursemaid whom the Ottos dismissed when they discovered her practicing black magic. Before she left, though, she gave young Gene a life-sized boy doll for his fourth birthday that she had crafted just for him. Some stories claim the servant was utterly devoted to Gene and made it for him out of love. Others paint a darker picture and claim the woman made the doll and then cursed it with voodoo in an act of revenge against the Ottos.

Author David Sloan, in his book *Robert the Doll*, dismisses both versions of the legend and offers a fascinating and thoroughly-researched alternative. Through contact with representatives of the Steiff toy company (the manufacturer of the original teddy bear in 1902), Sloan determined that Robert was actually a Steiff creation, most likely manufactured around 1904 in Germany. Originally designed as a clown doll and dressed in a pink and green Harlequin clown costume, Sloan believes the doll came to Key West when Minnie Otto, Gene's mother, returned from a trip to Germany in 1904 via the steamship *Graf Waldersee*. As Gene's fourth birthday was just a few months away, it would have made the perfect present.

As for the disgruntled servant and voodoo curse claims, Sloan sheds some additional light on the family's background that could help explain how the legends got started. First of all, Minnie Otto was herself a white Bahamian. Was she the inspiration behind the story of a Bahamian nursemaid who gave Gene a doll? Perhaps. It is also a known fact that the Ottos employed a domestic help couple, William and Emeline Abbott, whose lineage traced back to the Bahamas. Emeline lost a child sometime between 1900 and 1910. There remains some speculation, according to Sloan, that the child may have even been fathered by Thomas Otto. What makes this interesting is that several psychic sensitives have reported seeing the spirit that resides within the Robert doll and claim that it belongs to a light-skinned black child. Could Emeline Abbott, in an effort to keep the spirit of her lost child close, have somehow "trapped" it in Gene's doll—either with voodoo or some other mystical art? It's as viable a theory as any.

But none of this mattered at the time to young Gene. Regardless of where it came from or who did what to it, Gene took an immediate liking to his new companion and named him Robert after his own first name. From day one, Gene and Robert were inseparable. Robert accompanied Gene on family outings and shopping trips, sat at the dinner table in his own chair as Gene fed him bits of food, watched from a nearby perch in the bathroom as Gene took his baths, and of course was tucked in bed right alongside Gene at night. On those occasions when Gene dressed Robert in a replica sailor suit and then wore his own, the two of them could have been mistaken for twins.

Before long, however, the innocent, harmonious relationship of the boy and his doll took on a more disturbing nature. Gene had always talked to Robert, as any child would talk to a doll or favorite stuffed animal, but now the staff and Gene's parents were hearing a second voice talking back behind the closed door of Gene's room. This other voice was quite distinct; Gene's was often higher-pitched and querulous, while the second voice was deeper and more insistent. On one occasion, Gene's mother, upon hearing a loud, rather angry-sounding conversation and thudding going on in Gene's room, burst through the door to find Gene cowering in a corner of the room and Robert sitting in a chair looking down on the boy in a chastising manner. Another time, a loud commotion in the middle of the night brought the Ottos running to Gene's room where they found a terrible mess, furniture upended, and Gene hiding under his blanket in bed. When questioned as to what happened, the frightened boy answered, "Robert did it."

"Robert did it" became the standard answer from Gene as more and more strange occurrences began happening in the Otto household. Glassware and dishes were discovered thrown about and broken, furniture overturned, bedding tossed on the floor, clothes torn up, toys broken and mutilated, and servants locked out of rooms. More chillingly, some of the staff reported hearing giggling coming from Robert and seeing him running through the house. Not surprisingly, the staff turnover rate was high.

Family and friends knew what was going on, and one day Gene's great aunt tried to intervene by recommending that Robert be banished to the attic. Over Gene's mighty protests, his parents did pack Robert in a box and placed him in the attic, hoping that would quiet things down for a while. But apparently Robert had other plans. The very next day, the great aunt was found dead in her bed, the victim of an apparent stroke. Soon after, Robert was released from his attic prison and given back to Gene.

As Gene grew older, he decided to act on his innate artistic abilities and pursue a vocation as an artist. After a short stint at the University of Virginia, he went on to study at the Academy of Fine Arts in Chicago. After three years there, he attended the Arts Student League of New York, and from there went on to further study in Paris. While in Paris, Gene met Annette Parker, an accomplished pianist from Boston. The two young students hit it off instantly, and on May 3, 1930, were married. The newlyweds stayed in Paris for a few years until Annette finished her studies, after which they moved to New York where Gene painted and Annette performed regularly at the Rockefeller Center. This idyllic life lasted until 1945 when Gene's mother died and he was left as the sole inheritor of his childhood home in Key West.

While Anne wasn't thrilled about trading the bustle and excitement of New York City for the laid back placidity of Key West, she soon settled into a domestic routine that suited her. Gene became a celebrated artist on the island and spent most of his days painting in the turret room of the mansion, where the lighting was most favorable for his work. Neighbors and passersby on the street could often see Gene working on his latest creation through the turret's many windows. They also frequently saw someone else—or *something* else—looking back at them.

Robert.

From the moment he returned home and found his childhood companion stored away in the attic, Gene once again became enchanted with the doll and took up where he left off as a child, carrying it around with him, seating it at the dinner table, and perching it on a chair beside the bed he shared with Anne. He busied himself with making scaled down furniture for Robert and even made him new outfits, including another sailor suit and a pixie costume. Not surprisingly, Anne was not pleased with Gene's obsession with Robert and on more than one occasion tried to hide the doll away in the attic. But always, either through Gene's actions or some other way, Robert found his way back down to their living quarters.

As time went on, Gene's behavior became more eccentric—and Robert's antics became even more disturbing. Dinner guests were alarmed to hear demonic giggling and the sounds of footsteps coming from the upper rooms where Robert had been placed for the evening. Other visitors, if Robert was in the same room as them, reported seeing him change facial expressions, often in response to the current conversation. Neighborhood children reported seeing Robert turn his head and seemingly taunt them as he watched them from the turret window. Other witnesses claimed seeing the doll actually *run* from window to window.

The toll all of this was taking on Gene's and Anne's marriage became more and more apparent to those close to the couple. It was known that Gene would become upset whenever Anne would attempt to move Robert out of sight, and it was widely suspected that Gene was becoming increasingly cruel and abusive toward Anne, not in a physical sense, but mentally and emotionally. When confronted about his behavior, Gene resorted to his childhood response: "I didn't do it. Robert did it."

Gene died on June 24, 1974, after a lengthy and difficult battle with Parkinson's disease. It was widely rumored that instead of seeking comfort from his wife, he spent his last days in the attic room talking to Robert. After Gene's death, Anne was faced with the unpleasant prospect of being alone with Robert. And if the local stories are to be believed, it wasn't an amicable co-existence. Robert seemed more than distraught over losing his lifetime companion. He seemed angry, enraged even, and displayed his childishly bad temper by placing curses on visitors to the house, running around feverishly in the turret room, and appearing randomly and mysteriously in other rooms. To make matters worse, Anne tragically found out that Gene had left her nothing in his will but the house. Everything else went to his sister Mizpah—including all their shared antiques and artwork that could have kept her financially solvent. Faced with financial difficulties and an empty house that she shared with a very disturbing doll, Anne sold the house to her friend William Gaiser and moved back to Massachusetts where she lived for several more years before succumbing to cancer.

Gaiser in turn sold the house to his friends William and Myrtle Reuter in late 1974. Robert was still in the house, stored away upstairs, but would be causing mayhem and mischief soon enough. In the mid '70s, the house was rented out several times. Two men who were early tenants reported hearing strange noises coming from the room above. Sometimes it was like small children laughing; other times it was the sound of someone rummaging around. The men always went upstairs to investigate, and after a few such times they noticed that "the doll" had moved. At first they assumed one was pranking the other. But when Robert continued to appear in different locations and positions, they realized something else was happening, something they couldn't explain. They asked a friend of theirs, Malcolm, to come over and check it out. When Malcolm entered Robert's room, he immediately felt like he was entering some sort of force field. He also swore that Robert's expression changed in response to the conversation the three men were having. "There was some sort of intelligence there. The doll was listening to us."

A plumber who was on the premise one day reported hearing giggling behind him. When he turned around, Robert was on a different side of the room than where he had been when the plumber first arrived. Still another tenant reported that Robert locked him in the attic for days and then later cursed him with yellow fever.

Despite the stories she had heard, Myrtle Reuter actually took a liking to Robert. At least for a while. She kept him in her company for the six years she lived at the Otto house, and took him along to her new residence on Von Phister Street, where she often sat him on her front porch. But in 1994, when Myrtle appeared at the front desk of the Fort East Martello Museum to donate Robert to the museum, it was apparent her feelings toward her longtime companion had radically changed. "He's haunted," Myrtle flatly asserted to museum assistant director Joe Pais. "I can't stand him being in my house anymore." She then went on to tell the surprised museum employees how Robert frequently moved around her house all on his own. One time he even locked her inside a room. Myrtle thought this was in retribution for her locking him up once after his wandering got out of hand. Refusing to accept anything in exchange for the doll, she left Robert in the hands of new caretakers. Myrtle died a few months later.

Fort East Martello Museum

When Robert first arrived at the Fort East Martello Museum, his infamously creepy reputation led to his being placed in a back room, covered with a sheet alongside other items for eventual display. People could request an appointment to see Robert, but even then staff members would try to rearrange their own schedules so as to not be the ones working during those visits. Apparently, Robert didn't like this treatment. One evening, several employees reported seeing something white fly through the air, down a hallway, past an arch, and up a corridor. The curator in charge of Robert's area was a no-nonsense, non-superstitious woman who had pooh-poohed the stories of the flying doll. One day shortly after the incident happened, the curator didn't show up for work, yet her bicycle was still chained to the rack in front of the museum. No formal explanation was ever given for her sudden departure, but the staff later learned that she'd seen something in Robert's section of the building that sent her screaming and running in terror out of the museum and all the way home.

A change in curators also brought about a change in Robert's living quarters and he was shortly thereafter put on public display. To this day he can still be seen inside a plexiglass display case, sitting on a doll-sized wooden chair and clutching a stuffed lion nicknamed Leo. But Robert has certainly not "retired" quietly to his new surroundings. If anything, he's more active than ever.

"All of us who work with him have, at the very least, seen his facial expression change. Most of us have seen him move," related Thomas Locklear of Historic Tours of America and former Operations Manager for Key West's Ghosts and Gravestones Frightseeing Tour. More than once, museum staff members have reported hearing tapping noises by Robert's exhibit. When they've turned to look, they've seen the doll's hand pressed against the display glass.

One of the strangest stories from the museum comes from an employee who once cleaned Robert from top to bottom, put him back in his display case, turned off the lights, and locked the doors before leaving for the evening. The next day, the employee, who was the first to arrive at the museum, was amazed to see that several of the lights were on, including the one near Robert's case, and that Robert himself was in a different position than what the employee placed him in the previous evening. But most unsettling was the fresh coat of dust on Robert's shoes. It was almost as if Robert had been walking around the museum in the middle of the night.

Though the Fort East Martello Museum has been around for a long time (the building itself was built during the Civil War to defend against Confederate attacks) and contains many interesting items related to Key West military history, industry and art, it has become, for all intents and purposes, Robert's museum. And Robert reigns over his eclectic kingdom like a petulant prince. Visitors are asked right away when entering to please follow Robert's Rules: 1) You must say hello to him when you enter. 2) You must ask permission of him before taking a picture. 3) You must say *thank you* and *goodbye* when you leave. If you don't follow the rules, Robert may cause bad things to happen to you. A myriad of letters from people all over the country are taped to the wall behind Robert's display case, the writers apologizing to Robert for snapping his picture without asking, making fun of him, or for some other breach of etiquette for which they believe they are now paying the price.

Robert with letters from visitors

Robert's most common alleged activity is causing problems with electrical devices. Stories abound of cameras malfunctioning, batteries mysteriously running out, cell phones acting erratically, and lights flickering on and off. There have even been reports of pacemaker failures in Robert's presence. People who take pictures sometimes find that either all of their pictures turned out except those of Robert, or none of their pictures turned out *except* for those of Robert.

Thomas Locklear had his own technical mishap that he suspects Robert may have had something to do with. Locklear was taking pictures inside the museum one day with his cell phone camera. He had not asked Robert's permission because he wasn't taking pictures of Robert, just things in Robert's room. Before he left the premises, he noticed that his phone got extremely hot and then stopped working. When he took it to Verizon the next day, the service people told him the entire inside of the phone had burned up. They had never seen anything like it.

The Travel Channel also had an interesting experience with Robert. On location to film an episode of *Mysteries at the Museum* featuring Robert, the film crew couldn't even get started, as their best HD camera suddenly wouldn't work. They waited it out, thinking perhaps the difference in temperature between the cooler hotel and the warmer museum was causing the problem. Eventually, and inexplicably, the camera started working again and they shot their segment. But when the crew checked the film before packing up, they were surprised to see that it was blank! They attempted to have another HD camera shipped to the museum, but the shipping cost was so high they decided to just use their back up camera. Before filming this time, however, the crew apologized to Robert and asked him nicely if they could reshoot the episode using this new camera. Hoping for the best, the crew then went ahead and got the coverage they needed without any further problems. The episode aired on January 11, 2011.

Robert apparently can cause trouble from afar as well. It's a wonder that David Sloan ever completed his book

Robert the Doll, as he had four hard drives crash on him during its writing. Technicians were able to recover everything except the book files. Backup manuscripts also mysteriously disappeared.

Despite all the stories of mischief, menace and mayhem attributed to him, Robert continues to draw an endless stream of visitors to Fort East Martello. The museum is open daily (except Christmas) from 9:30 a.m. to 4:30 p.m. for those souls brave enough to visit in person. The rest of us can visit Robert at either his website or Facebook page. Permission doesn't seem to be necessary.

The Artist's House, Robert's abode for many decades, is also open to the public. Now a popular bed and breakfast, guests still occasionally report strange noises, objects moving by themselves, and a feeling of being watched. Others have reported seeing a phantom female, who is believed by some to be the ghost of Anne Otto. The theory goes that Anne has come back to protect the house from Robert's evil influence.

The Artist's House

Whatever is behind Robert the Doll's influence, activities, or other alleged powers remains a mystery. Many contend, as discussed earlier, that Robert is the embodiment of a voodoo curse, most likely put in place by William and/or Emeline Abbott. Others insist he is possessed by an evil spirit. Still others think Robert isn't so much evil as simply mischievous, the acting out of a little boy trapped in an inanimate object. Another theory suggests that Gene Otto projected so much energy on the doll as a child—much of it negative—that now his spirit and Robert are one. While much speculation exists and will for some time, when it comes to the odd occurrences that happen around this century-old doll, one thing can be stated pretty confidently:

Robert did it.

Chapter 2

Annabelle

Warning, Positively Do Not Open.

– The sign on Annabelle's glass case in the Occult Museum

The decade of the 1970s was dawning, and Donna was just about to turn 28. For her birthday, Donna's mother bought her a large, antique Raggedy Ann doll that she had found at a local hobby store. Donna loved the doll and thought it would make a great decoration in her bedroom. The next morning, Donna propped the doll up on her made bed and, satisfied that all was right in her pleasant-but-routine world, went off to her nurse's job without another thought about her new bedroom companion.

All *was* right at first. But shortly after receiving the doll, Donna and her roommate, Angie, who was also a nurse, started noticing something strange. The doll was never in quite the same position when they came home as when they left in the morning. Donna usually left the doll with its legs outstretched and its arms off to the side. But when they came home, the doll's legs would be crossed or its arms would be resting in its lap. After a few days of this, the roommates "tested" the doll. They deliberately crossed the doll's arms and legs before they left for work. Sure enough, when they came home the doll was sitting there with its appendages uncrossed.

Soon it wasn't just its arms and legs the doll seemed to be moving. It started moving *itself* to different locations in the apartment. Several times the women would come home to find the doll sitting on the living room sofa even though Donna had left it in her bedroom with the door shut in the morning. On one particularly eerie occasion, Donna and Angie came home to find themselves greeted by the doll *kneeling* on a chair by the front door. How it could kneel mystified the women, as they couldn't get the doll to remain upright when they tried themselves to make it kneel.

In addition to moving freely around the apartment, the doll was now doing something else that made the women uneasy, to say the least: it was leaving them written messages. On small pieces of parchment paper, written in pencil in a child's scrawl, would be the words "Help Us" or "Help Lou," Lou being Angie's fiancée. Most troubling was the fact that neither Donna nor Angie owned any parchment paper. There were also no pencils to be found anywhere in the apartment.

Assuming at this point that someone was breaking into their apartment and playing a nasty prank on them, the roommates left marks on the doors and windows and arranged the rugs in a certain fashion so they could tell if someone had been in the apartment while they were gone. All their attempts were for naught, though, as none of their markings were ever disturbed.

One night in the midst of all these happenings, Donna and Angie came home and found the doll, to their relief, on

Donna's bed where it belonged. But upon closer inspection, they saw that the doll had blood on the back of its hand and three drops of blood on its chest. Having ruled out a prankster and knowing with certainty that they weren't both imagining things, the women reached out to a medium for help.

The medium told them that a little girl named Annabelle Higgins had died on the property years before the apartment building was built. Annabelle was still there in spirit form, and she chose to be in this apartment because she felt Donna and Angie could understand her better than the other busy grown-ups in the building. She had been moving the doll around, she explained, as a way to get the women's attention. She just wanted to be loved, she told them through the medium. Then she asked if she could move into the doll and stay with them. Compassionate by nature, the two nurses agreed to the spirit's request. After that, they referred to the doll as "Annabelle."

Unfortunately, the one-big-happy-family scenario talked about at the séance didn't really pan out. For one thing, Annabelle seemed to have a problem with Angie's fiancée, Lou. From the beginning, Lou had never liked the doll. It felt "evil" to him, and on more than one occasion he told Donna she should get rid of it. During the six-week period the doll was in the apartment, Lou started experiencing recurring nightmares. One "dream" in particular confirmed his judgment about Annabelle.

After falling into a very deep sleep, Lou had what could be called an out-of-body experience. He remembered seeing himself wake up and feeling like something was terribly wrong. When he looked around, though, everything in his room seemed normal. Then he saw it. At the foot of his bed was the Annabelle doll—and it was moving toward him. Fear crept over him as he watched Annabelle glide up his body, move over his chest, and stop at his neck. Then it moved its arms out to both sides of Lou's neck and started to strangle him. Lou thrashed and writhed in agony as he tried to push the doll away, but it was like trying to push away a concrete wall. The cloth Raggedy Ann doll simply wouldn't budge. Lou struggled until he finally passed out. The next morning the doll was gone, and other than a horrifying memory, there was no evidence that anything out of the ordinary had occurred. Lou was certain, though, that what he experienced had not been a dream, and it only strengthened his resolve to convince Donna to get rid of Annabelle.

It seemed to make Annabelle's resolve stronger, too.

Shortly after the "dream" incident, Lou was at the women's apartment going over some last-minute details with Angie regarding a trip he was taking in the morning. It was about eleven o'clock at night when the two of them suddenly heard noises coming from Donna's room. Thinking perhaps someone had broken in, Lou quietly approached the closed bedroom door. He waited until the noises stopped and then forcefully opened the door and turned on the light. No one was there other than Annabelle, and she was laying haphazardly in a corner. Lou walked into the room for a closer look at things when he suddenly had the distinct feeling that someone was behind him. He turned and then doubled over in pain as something hot and sharp cut across his torso. Hearing his yells, Angie ran in and saw him clutching his chest, his shirt torn and blood running through his fingers. She guided him back to the living room and inspected Lou's wounds. She couldn't believe her eyes. Claw marks—three vertical and four horizontal—were scratched across Lou's chest as clear as day.

Surprisingly, the marks cleared up incredibly fast. They were half gone by the next day, and fully gone the following. But that was the last straw needed to convince Donna and Angie that Annabelle wasn't exactly what she claimed to be. Afraid they would be laughed at or considered crazy if they went to just anyone with their story, they contacted an Episcopal priest they knew from a nearby junior college. They trusted him and it turned out their instincts were good. Father Lawrence listened to the whole account—about Annabelle moving around, the strange messages, the spirit contact, and Lou's cuts—and told them he believed them, but that he felt he should contact his superior, as his own experience in such matters was minimal.

When Father Edward heard the story from his young compatriot, he suspected that they weren't dealing with a simple ghost, especially given the physical attack on Lou. So he referred the case to Ed and Lorraine Warren, renowned demonologists whose work he had heard about, and asked if they would assess the case before he took any further action. The Warrens accepted the case and met with Donna, Angie, and Lou shortly thereafter.

It didn't take the Warrens long to conclude that there was indeed a spirit attached to the Annabelle doll, but it wasn't that of a little girl named Annabelle Higgins. It was something inhuman—demonic. While Lorraine walked through the apartment to discern spirit activity (Lorraine is a clairvoyant and a light-trance medium), Ed explained to the roommates that ordinary ghosts don't have the capability of teleportation, writing messages, manifesting blood, and, particularly, physically attacking someone with the intensity that happened to Lou. He recommended that they call in a priest immediately for an exorcism. Lorraine agreed, saying that she did indeed discern a spirit in the apartment, one whose behavior was unpredictable.

While they waited for Father Edward to arrive, the Warrens further explained that the entity in their apartment had tricked them from the start. It moved the doll around to pique their curiosity and gain their attention. Then, when it had that, it used the doll to instill fear and even injury. "This is the nature of the inhuman spirit," said Ed. "It's negative, it enjoys inflicting pain." But making matters much worse was when the women called in the medium. The entity "came through" as a lost, innocent little girl when in reality it was a lying, treacherous demonic spirit that played off the nurses' compassion to gain a further foothold into their lives. What it was looking for—and what it received—was permission to move into the Raggedy Ann doll. "It was like handing a maniac a loaded gun," Ed told them.

So, was the doll *possessed?* Donna and Angie wanted to know. The Warrens told them no, demonic spirits don't possess objects, they possess people. And eventually, that's what the entity in their apartment hoped to do: possess one or all of them. It had a special hatred for Lou because he posed a threat. He suspected there was something evil about the doll and was determined to do something about it. Unfortunately, that made him a target for the demon.

"We've seen this claw mark in other cases," Ed told Lou. "It's a telltale sign of an inhuman presence." Ed further said that Lou was lucky that's all that happened to him. Given another week or two, any of the occupants of the apartment could have been killed.

By this time, Father Edward arrived at the apartment and agreed to perform an exorcism-blessing ritual, which consisted of a five-minute prayer being said in each room. When he was done, he also blessed everyone present, after which Lorraine confirmed that no negative spirits were in the apartment. For Donna, Angie, and Lou, the nightmare was over. But just to be sure, Donna asked Ed if he would take the doll with him. Gift or not, she wanted nothing to do with it anymore. Ed agreed and the Warrens took their leave with Annabelle in tow.

The good news was that Donna, Angie, and Lou were now free of the demonic spirit that had invaded their apartment for six weeks. The bad news was, it was still attached to Annabelle.

The Warrens soon discovered this while driving home after the exorcism. Suspecting that perhaps the negative entity was still hanging around, Ed and Lorraine put the doll in the back seat and purposely chose not to drive home on the Interstate—just in case Annabelle caused problems.

Their hunch was right. They no sooner got going when they both felt an intense sense of hatred directed at them. Then, going into a curve in the road, their car swerved and stalled, nearly causing them to collide with oncoming traffic. This happened a couple of times before Ed reached into his bag, took out a vial of holy water, and tossed it on the doll while making the sign of the cross over it. This seemed to work, as the Warrens experienced no further disturbances on the ride home.

For the next few days, Ed kept Annabelle in a chair in his home office. Ed reported that she levitated several times but seemed to grow weary of that game fairly quickly when he didn't show a reaction to it. After that she branched out and moved around from room to room. It wasn't unusual for the Warrens to lock Annabelle in one room before they left on business in the morning only to find her sitting in an easy chair in another when they returned home. During this time, the Warrens also reported seeing a mysterious black cat in their home. But unlike a typical stray, this cat—undoubtedly a friend of Annabelle's—would suddenly materialize next to the doll, slink around the room while investigating Ed's books and curios, and then go back over to Annabelle and dematerialize from the head down.

One day a Catholic priest, Father Mark, came over to discuss some business with Ed. He noticed Annabelle sitting in a chair and asked Ed about this newest addition to his office. Ed related the whole story to him, after which Father Mark picked up the doll and said nonchalantly, "You're just a rag doll, Annabelle. You can't hurt anything." Ed laughed and told him that was probably the wrong thing to say, but the priest just shrugged and tossed Annabelle back down in the chair. Later, as he was preparing to leave, Lorraine urged him to be especially careful on the car ride home, keeping to herself that she had discerned trouble-in-the-making for the priest. A short while later, Father Mark called the Warrens. He was back at the rectory, but wanted Lorraine to know that her instincts had been right: his brakes had failed and he had been nearly killed in a car accident.

On another occasion, a police detective came over to Ed's office to get help with a witchcraft-related murder case he was working on. While in the middle of the meeting, Lorraine called Ed to come upstairs to take a long-distance telephone call. Before he left, Ed told the detective to feel free to look around but not to touch any of the objects in the office, as some had been involved in demonic activity. About five minutes later, the detective rushed into the room upstairs where Ed was, trembling and pale. When Ed asked him what was wrong, the detective answered haltingly, "The doll, the rag doll is *real* . . ."

The Warrens eventually had a special glass case built for Annabelle, which she is still in to this day and which is viewable to the public in the Occult Museum located on the Warrens' property. In a recent interview, Lorraine explained: "As least as it sits, we know where it resides. It isn't out into the world causing harm to others. We have a Catholic priest who performs a binding prayer around the doll which acts as a blockade . . . Think of it as similar to an electric dog fence—keeping the dog within set boundaries."

But if you challenge a really vicious, vindictive, and intelligent dog, even if it's within declared boundaries, you may still become that dog's chew toy. This is what a young man tragically discovered when visiting the Occult Museum one day shortly after Annabelle was encased. Having arrived on a motorcycle with his girlfriend, the man listened as Ed told the story about the doll. Afterward, he went over to Annabelle's case and started banging on it and yelling at the doll to put scratches on him like she did on other people. Ed quickly ushered the man out. The Warrens later learned that the young man and his girlfriend had been laughing about Annabelle on the ride home when suddenly the man lost control of the motorcycle and crashed head on into a tree. The impact killed him instantly and put his girlfriend in the hospital for a year.

As for Annabelle, she sits contentedly in her glass case—waiting for someone to open it.

Chapter 3

Mandy

"Strange things happen when Mandy is about."

– Quesnel Museum website

Ruth Stubbs remembered clearly the day she first laid eyes on Mandy. Ruth was the curator at the Quesnel Museum in British Columbia in 1991 when a woman walked in wanting to donate an old doll that she said belonged to her grandmother. The woman seemed particularly eager to get rid of it. "She practically plopped the doll down on my desk," recalled Ruth in a 1995 article in the *Quesnel Advocate*. The woman went on to explain that she was donating the doll—Mandy—because she didn't want her daughter to play with it, given its age and deteriorating condition. There was another reason as well, but Ruth wouldn't find that out until a bit later.

Ruth accepted the doll, although at first there wasn't a lot to like about it. It was indeed old, a porcelain model believed to have been made in England or Germany between 1910 and 1920. Its soft body was torn in multiple places and its clothing was stained and grubby. Most unflattering was a large crack running down the side of its face which made one eye appear to leer independently of the other. Chipped paint and other smaller marks and cracks added to Mandy's overall battered-child-like appearance.

Mandy

In keeping with procedure, museum workers first put Mandy in a clear plastic covering for 48 hours to determine if any insects had infested her body. The effect of being shrouded in plastic wrap only intensified Mandy's eeriness and "was creepy, to say the least," remembered Ruth. Other staff members reported similar thoughts and feelings when around Mandy those first couple of days.

After her quarantine ended, Mandy was then photographed from various angles and in different positions as part of the cataloging process. The photographer and her boyfriend who was along to help reported feeling uneasy during the shoot, but completed the session without any problems. The next day, however, when they returned to their photo lab they were astonished to find the room in total disarray. Pens, pencils, and other items had been thrown and scattered all around as if, in Ruth's words, "a small child had had a temper tantrum." A bit later, the photographer went into her darkroom to develop Mandy's photos. She came back out looking pale and flustered, and told fellow staffers that while she was in the darkroom she heard a loud sigh behind her followed by something suddenly falling off a shelf.

Not knowing quite what to do yet with their newly-acquired artifact, museum workers placed Mandy in a makeshift case that faced the entrance doors. It wasn't long before patrons reported feeling like the doll's eyes followed them around the room, or that they saw Mandy's eyes move or blink. Many others reported feeling an inexplicable sadness after viewing the doll. Still other visitors found that their cameras mysteriously malfunctioned around Mandy. One woman claimed the light on her camera went on and off every five seconds until she left the room, at which point it went back to working normally again.

One day Ruth invited a photographer from the *Cariboo Observer* to come and take some pictures of Mandy. Afterward he called to report that he had no photos, as the contact sheet had been chewed up in the developer. That had never happened before, he said. *Quesnel Advocate* photographer Seth Gotro claimed that when he took pictures of Mandy, he had the surreal experience of seeing her turn her head away from the lens. When he finally lined up the shot he wanted, he swore that the doll smiled at him right as the flash hit her face.

Reports of strange occurrences were coming in fast and furious by now. Not only were visitors to the museum seeing and feeling things they couldn't explain, staff members were also experiencing oddities. Lunches would disappear from the refrigerator and show up later in desk drawers; pens, pencils, books, and other assorted sundries went missing with regularity; footsteps could be heard at night by workers who thought they were alone.

Ruth was well aware of all the stories being reported, but in spite of her admitted curiosity, she maintained a professional skepticism around the staff. But then one day a retired curator from Surrey visited the Quesnel Museum. This man was known for his ability to determine things about artifacts, or to "read" their histories, just by touching them. (In paranormal jargon this is the psychic gift of psychometry.) He picked up Mandy and immediately felt cold chills race through his body. He set her back down and stated that the doll had seen a lot of abuse throughout its existence.

Ruth's curiosity now had the better of her, and so she reached out to the doll's previous owner, hoping for a little more background information. The woman shared this story with Ruth: Mandy had originally belonged to the woman's grandmother. When she (the donor) took possession of it, she stored it in her basement. Soon strange things started happening. At night the woman kept hearing a baby crying in the basement. But whenever she went down to look, all she found was an open window and a breeze blowing in.

The woman would close the window, go back upstairs, and the next night would hear the crying again. Never was a real baby ever found, either in the basement or outside the house. The only "baby" on the premises was Mandy. And from the day Mandy was donated to the museum, the crying in the woman's home stopped.

"Now, this is what she *told* me," Ruth said cautiously. "True? Who knows."

While the greater part of Mandy's background remains a mystery, her current status as the star of the Quesnel Museum is undisputed. Mandy the Doll draws crowds of visitors year-round, many hoping to catch a blinking eye, a turning head, or a moving finger. Some may hope for a bigger story to tell back home, like how their camera battery suddenly drained the instant it got near her. Unlike Robert, the haunted doll of Key West, Mandy does not seem to curse her visitors. At most, she may share with them an overwhelming feeling of sadness or maybe a bit of mischief. Her true secrets she keeps to herself.

* * *

Would you like to see Mandy up close and personal? The Quesnel Museum is open seven days a week. Current information about exhibits and operating hours can be found on its website (www.quesnelmuseum.ca).

Chapter 4

Letta

*"You could hear the wood creaking as it turned [its head]
and looked directly at the camera."*

– Kisha, Australian psychic

It had been years since Kerry Walton gave a thought about the legendary haunted house in his hometown of Wagga Wagga in New South Wales. But when he returned home in 1972 to attend his grandmother's funeral, those boyhood memories flooded over him once again. However, this time while looking at the dilapidated house, he wasn't so much scared as he was intrigued. Now a collectibles dealer, Kerry found himself thinking that the old building might just contain something more valuable than a few ghosts.

Pushing his childhood fears aside, Kerry headed over to the long-abandoned abode, found an opening to the cellar, and ventured in with flashlight in hand, hoping to find some antique glass treasures. Decades of accumulated dust and cobwebs in the darkened dwelling made finding anything a challenge, but suddenly Kerry's light swept across something startling, so startling, in fact, that Kerry jumped up and nearly knocked himself out on an overhead beam. What Kerry had seen in the dim light of his torch was a face, a face that he first thought belonged to a small dead child. Upon closer inspection, Kerry saw that it was actually a large doll. But this was no child's baby doll. The thing, resembling a marionette, was decidedly male, with piercing dark eyes, a large hooked nose, and an elongated, jutting chin that made its overall appearance rather grotesque. Nonetheless, Kerry gathered the doll up and made his exit from the cellar before any more surprises could jump out at him.

During the long drive home, Kerry and his brother had the doll in a sack in the back seat of their van. It was a bit of a disturbing trip, Kerry recalled, because whenever the headlights of oncoming cars shone into the van, it looked like the doll was moving within the sack. Kerry and his brother both reported hearing strange sounds coming from the sack as well, but tried to make light of it in order to drive home safely. Jokingly, they attributed the words "letta me out" to the doll, and that led to the doll henceforth being called Letta.

When Kerry arrived home with Letta, the strangeness continued. The Waltons' family dog, a normally mild-mannered corgi, immediately tried to attack the doll in a frenzy of barking and snapping, behavior completely adverse to anything Kerry had witnessed in his dog before. Relatives and friends remarked how the doll repulsed them, and how its eyes always seemed to be following them. Kerry's children actually played with the doll during the day, but one night when Letta was left in their bedroom, the children woke up screaming, prompting Kerry to put the doll in storage in the basement, where it remained for five years.

Letta

Letta may have been out of sight, but he wasn't out of mind. Even after five years, Kerry's curiosity about the doll's origins remained strong, and he finally decided to get an expert evaluation. He took the doll to the Australian Museum in Sydney, where he was told the doll was between 175 to 250 years old and most likely the work of an Eastern European gypsy craftsman. Gypsies at that time believed in spirit transference and often created dolls to act as sanctuaries for human souls after death. The doll's age could be pinpointed from the nails in the bottoms of its shoes. Other details about the doll were equally fascinating, such as its having human hair and simulated blood veins etched into its eyes. But perhaps most intriguing about the doll was its "brain." Visible when the top of the doll's head was lifted up, this replication of a human brain was described by Kerry as looking "something like the color of wet newspaper."

Thinking that the age and uniqueness of the doll might make it valuable, Kerry advertised the doll as being for sale. It didn't take long for a generous offer to come in, but when Kerry arrived at the buyer's house and tried to take Letta out of the car, he found to his amazement that he physically couldn't. "I was glued to my seat. No matter how hard I tried, I couldn't move." Sitting there in his car with the rain pounding down, Kerry realized that for whatever reason, he and Letta were to remain together.

While many people found Letta hideous and creepy and preferred not to be in his company, Kerry got on just fine with the antique effigy. In fact, having Letta around started to be a blessing instead of a curse. Having struggled financially for some time, Kerry was now pleasantly surprised to see his collectibles business turning profitable. Not only that, he and Letta were increasingly being asked to appear on television talk shows and at various fairs and exhibitions. When Brisbane psychic Kisha heard about this unusual story, she offered to investigate further and held a séance during which she pronounced that the doll harbored the memory of a tragedy and that it "felt" sadness over a child who had drowned. The reason it rained so often when Letta was outside (which it always seemed to do) was due to the association with water and drowning.

Kisha, Kerry, and Letta were soon to appear together on *State Affair*, an Australian television news show, in 1981.

Before the taping, Letta was brought into Kisha's office so the camera crew could determine the best way to film the two together during the segment. Kisha recalled that encounter: "When the doll arrived at my office—in the rain—a painting immediately fell from the wall and the clock stopped." Undeterred, the psychic placed the doll in her lap while the cameramen lined up their equipment. Then something very strange and unexpected happened. The doll wriggled in her lap! She tried to convince the crew what had just happened, but they had a hard time believing her. "Oh, c'mon! That's impossible," one of the men said. But then something happened that made them believers: Letta, ever so slowly, moved his head. "You could hear the wood creaking as it turned and looked directly at the camera," Kisha recalled. And then just at that moment a light bulb blew. One of the cameramen turned a deathly shade of white and bolted from the room. Kisha took the opportunity to tune into Letta to learn more about the doll's history and meaning.

"As I tuned into the doll, I discovered the soul of a six-year-old boy trapped within the wooden vessel. The child had drowned during a storm in an isolated area of Romania. His father, overcome with grief, fashioned a life-size figure in readiness for the ceremony of soul transference. The child has been imprisoned for centuries. He's confused and frightened," Kisha told her television audience. She also claimed to learn that the doll was brought to Australia by immigrants and buried in the cellar of an old house.

The story of the haunted gypsy doll and Kisha's revelations quickly got around thanks to exposure in a national magazine. A group of American paranormal investigators who caught wind of the story traveled to Australia and conducted a séance of their own with Kerry's permission. Their results were good: Letta supposedly spoke through them at the séance and confirmed everything Kisha had learned, plus this little tidbit for Kerry. "The Americans told me I would never be able to get rid of the doll," he revealed. "At least that explains why I couldn't get out of the car."

The Americans immediately wanted to take Letta on a U.S. talk show circuit, but Kerry opted instead to do an Australian tour with locally known psychics and astrologers. The tour was very popular, especially as there was always the chance that something out-of-the-ordinary would occur. At one stop in Brisbane in April 1981, Letta was put on display at a shopping center amidst a large crowd in broad daylight. As the curtains to the exhibit were pulled aside, women started screaming in the audience. One passed out, and another vomited, all due to extreme fear. Kisha speculated afterwards that Letta projected those negative feelings because he didn't like being there, didn't like being an exhibition.

At another stop on the tour, this one drawing about 200 people, Kerry had just placed Letta on the stage and was inviting the crowd to gather around when, again, a woman started screaming. As the startled crowd looked toward the stage, the source of the woman's distress revealed itself: Letta was moving his head!

Seeing the doll move on its own was something Kerry had seen before. "For a long time I had him sitting in an old rocking chair upstairs. His arms and legs would move on their own." Kerry's wife has claimed to have seen the doll change his physical appearance, one day looking sad, the next happy and smiling. "I know it sounds weird," she said, "but he does change his facial expressions."

In 1994, Kerry and Letta were preparing to do another television interview, this one for the Australian show *The Extraordinary*, which broadcast episodes of true paranormal events. As Kerry was sitting in the studio, holding Letta in his lap and answering the interviewer's questions, one of the large spotlights blew out behind him. After a few chaotic moments during which the crew fixed the lighting, Kerry calmly explained that bulbs blowing out occurs quite frequently when Letta's around.

When talking about the doll at a later venue, Kisha had her own viewpoint as to why that particular blow-out occurred on the set of *The Extraordinary*. She believed that Letta "remembered" the ridiculing from the cameramen in her office years back when she tried to tell them the doll moved in her lap. So when he was placed in a similar setting with cameras and lights, he got angry and acted on that memory. As Kisha explained: "He's real. He has the energy of someone trapped in him. He has memories. He would feel the emotions."

To this day, many unexplainable phenomena continue to happen around Letta. As previously noted, it rains frequently when he's taken around outside. All dogs, not just Kerry's, will bark and snap fiercely at him. Pictures will often fall off walls when he is brought into a room. And many people report feeling sad and afraid when they see him. Kerry has said that on several occasions service people that had been called to his house suddenly refused to enter when they neared the threshold, even though they had no knowledge that the doll was inside. "They just felt an evil presence and refused to come inside," Kerry said.

Over the years, Kerry has grown comfortable with having Letta around. In a 2002 television interview, Kerry said that he and his wife both believe that Letta has brought good fortune into their lives and that the doll is "not for sale at any cost," despite some very generous offers for it, one as high as $10,000. Perhaps part of Kerry's reluctance comes from the warnings he's received from several mediums who have told him he must never try to get rid of the doll or he will be beset with bad luck. Regardless of the reasons why, Letta remains in Kerry Walton's possession.

Or is it the other way around?

Chapter 5

Claire

"I want answers for why she is what she is."

– Jill Phillips-Lingen

Jill was used to receiving gifts from Miss Marian, a beloved family friend and Jill's former Sunday school teacher. In the past the older woman had dropped by and given Jill stuffed animals, little figurines, and other toys. But on this particular day, eight-year-old Jill was given the most memorable gift yet—a dated but unblemished porcelain doll. Miss Marian said she thought the doll looked just like Jill when she was younger and that's why she wanted her to have it.

Although Jill was a tomboy who enjoyed playing more with Teenage Mutant Ninja Turtles and Transformers than with dolls, she graciously accepted the gift from her friend and placed it in a child-sized rocking chair she had in her bedroom. She named the doll Claire. On the outside, Claire was an ordinary-looking, even pretty, doll. Dark brown hair hung down from her head in loose curls, framing a cream-colored complexion, rosy cheeks, pink lips, and dark brown eyes. She wore a peachy-pink-and-cream dress adorned with an apron and ruffled underskirt. On her feet she wore removable black Mary Jane shoes. Claire's head, arms, hands, and legs from the knee down were porcelain. Her body was made from a soft, stuffed fabric.

Jill soon found out, however, that Claire's pleasant outward appearance was only masking a darker essence. From the start, Jill remembered feeling uneasy around Claire. Playing in her bedroom with the doll nearby, she couldn't help but feel that Claire was watching her like a prison guard might watch over an inmate, ready to pounce at any indication of an infraction.

But it was one evening when Jill was reading a book (of ghost stories, ironically) that something happened in Claire's presence that impressed itself deeply on Jill's eight-year-old mind. On Jill's dresser was a musical carousel horse. All of a sudden it sprang to life, not just emitting an odd note from, say, a floor vibration, but actually playing its entire song while the little horse figurine glided up and down to the music, just as it would had it been fully wound. Jill watched the scene before her in astonishment, knowing that what she was seeing was impossible. After a few moments, the music and the horse stopped as suddenly as they had started.

Now, any other child would have run screaming from the room to find her parents. But Jill had actually seen scary—scarier, even—things before in her childhood house. One was an entity she called Shadow Man, a black, faceless phantom that had appeared to her many times over the years. (And who appeared in later years to Jill's sister-in-law and other visitors.) When Jill had tried to convince her parents of Shadow Man's existence, they hadn't believed her, so she didn't think they'd believe her story about the music box either and so kept it to herself. Recalling the incident later as an adult, Jill said that at the time she really didn't associate the carousel incident with Claire. She just assumed it was caused by some "other spirit" that resided in the house.

Soon after that, "the voice" started happening. For several intense nights, Jill was startled awake by a woman's voice that seemed to be mere inches from her head, shouting, "Jill! Wake up!" Jill would jump out of bed only to find her bedroom empty. This not only happened to Jill, but also to her brother down the hall. Eventually the shouting voice died down and happened only periodically to Jill and her brother as the years went on. After the two of them moved out of the house, the unseen woman began screaming at Jill's father as he slept, and reportedly still does.

There may not have been any evidence linking Claire to "the voice," but other things started happening that cast the doll in a more troublesome light. Objects would disappear only to be found later on the floor in front of Claire. Jill would repeatedly put one of her belongings in one spot and then find it had been moved—to a spot closer to Claire. A ring went missing once and Jill found it in the doll's pocket. An unfamiliar perfume scent would, from time to time, pervade the bedroom, yet a source for the smell could never be found. It also wasn't unusual to see books inexplicably fall off shelves near Claire.

These things alone, while upsetting, were not necessarily terror-inducing. But one night something did happen that catapulted Claire from creepy to horrifying. It started when Jill was awakened by a rhythmic thumping sound in her bedroom. She groggily sat up and, aided by the eerie glow of a nightlight, saw what was making the noise: Claire's rocking chair, which was rocking back and forth on its own.

Now fully awake, Jill couldn't move her eyes off of Claire, although if she had, perhaps she wouldn't be haunted by nightmares to this day. Because the next thing that happened was a nightmare itself. The doll's feet slowly and deliberately turned themselves from a pointed-out position to a pointed-up position. And then the doll turned its head and looked straight at Jill. On some sort of hellish cue, all four of Jill's music boxes then turned on to provide a chaos of creepy background noise. Finally finding her voice, Jill screamed for her parents. The music boxes stopped, but Claire still stared defiantly at Jill.

That was enough for Jill to decide Claire needed to be put away. Although she couldn't find it within herself to actually get rid of the doll, she did pack it up in a box and placed it in the back of a storage closet, where it remained untouched until Jill was well into her adult years.

Jill came to learn some years later that Claire's time spent with Miss Marian was marked with mystery as well. Miss Marian admitted that she was not sure where the doll came from—she discovered it while cleaning out a closet one day, and could not recall ever having received it from anyone. She put it on display on a shelf, and soon thereafter strange things started happening in her house. For one thing, the doll didn't stay on the shelf. It reportedly moved on its own to different seating areas throughout the house.

Disembodied voices and footsteps could be heard coming from the basement; cigar smoke would materialize out of the blue; and glass would be heard to shatter, yet nothing was ever found broken. Miss Marian also claimed that sometimes at night invisible hands would tuck her into bed.

Whether or not the doll was the cause of all this strange phenomena was uncertain, as Miss Marian believed her house was haunted anyway by the spirits of the victims of a train accident that occurred in 1900 and which claimed the lives of 38 people. The awful event—the train plunged into a swollen creek—happened less than a mile away from her house.

In 2011, Claire's story caught the attention of author and radio show personality Tim Weisberg, host of *Spooky Southcoast*, a popular on-air program about paranormal topics. Tim was doing research for a book about haunted objects and asked Jill if he could run some experiments on the doll. Jill agreed and sent Claire to him via UPS, the first time Claire had been anywhere other than the back of a closet in 18 years.

When Tim first took Claire out of the packaging, the needle on his EMF (electromagnetic field) detector spiked, but quickly fell back to its base level and did not move again in subsequent testings. EVP (electronic voice phenomena) testing yielded no results either. However, one night Tim heard distinct male and female voices coming from his home office where he had placed Claire. When he went in to investigate, the voices stopped. Tim recounts these events and more, including Claire's affinity for raising the thermostat, in his now-published book, *Haunted Objects:*

Stories of Ghosts on Your Shelf, which he co-authored with Christopher Balzano.

No longer banished to a closet, Claire currently lives with a friend of Jill's in a haunted Victorian house in Atlanta. The friend is a Houngan, a male voodoo priest, and keeps Claire in check along with the rest of the spirits in his home.

Jill harbors no ill will toward her creepy childhood companion, and recently reflected on her experience in a rather positive light: "Claire will always be both a special and terrifying memory from my childhood. She's the reason I believe what I believe when it comes to spirituality and it's helped shaped my religious beliefs . . . She's one reason I delve into the paranormal as much as I do. I want answers for why she is what she is."

Chapter 6

Peggy

"In all my years of curiosity and research, I thought I pretty much understood most of what I encountered, and the abilities and limitations of the spirit world. Peggy, however, seems to push the boundaries of what I considered to be 'paranormal activity . . .'"

– Jayne Harris, Lead Investigator at HD Paranormal Research

The woman was distraught. She'd been experiencing chronic headaches, debilitating nausea, and terrifying nightmares. She was plagued with a continual sense of dread, and couldn't shake the feeling that there was an "unearthly presence" in her home. She knew the source of all this anguish, and she wanted it gone, she told paranormal investigator Jayne Harris. Please take it, she asked. *Please take the doll away.*

The doll in question was a large little girl doll with short blonde hair and vivid blue eyes. The woman told Jayne that no matter what room she hid the doll in, she was still tormented by nightmares and health problems. She had even called in a priest, but nothing he did helped. At her wit's end, the woman googled "haunted dolls" and came across Jayne's website. Hearing the woman's incredible story, Jayne was intrigued and agreed to take the doll.

That was in September 2014. Since then, Jayne has chronicled her investigation of the doll on her website Haunted-Dolls.com, Facebook page, and in a series of YouTube videos. One major breakthrough came in March 2015, when psychic medium Chris Crocker informed Jayne that he had made contact with an entity in the doll after studying her images. He learned that the doll's spirit was named Peggy. She had been born in 1946 and died of an asthma attack. When Chris asked her if she was happy, Peggy replied that she was not, that she was angry. Why? Chris persisted. "Not Christian," came her reply. Unknown to Chris at the time, Jayne had received 21 emails from viewers that suggested she take the cross off from around the doll's neck. They "felt" she didn't like it.

What has made Peggy somewhat of an Internet celebrity is that scores of people have come forward to share feelings, dreams, and tangible events they've experienced after looking at the doll's image or watching her in a video. Unfortunately, many of the experiences they've described have been negative. Jayne stated recently that over 80 people have complained of chest pains, headaches, and other illnesses after taking a look at Peggy. Others have reported their computers freezing up, lightbulbs suddenly blowing out, or their rooms going cold, sometimes just at the mention of the doll.

Four different psychic mediums have studied Peggy so far, and all say that she is restless and frustrated. They also believe she had been persecuted in her life, and very possibly was a Jewish Holocaust victim. While many offers have come from other psychics to take Peggy off Jayne's hands, Jayne is committed to continuing her work with the doll. In every case she takes on, Jayne starts out as a skeptic and looks first for rational explanations to alleged paranormal activity. One or two mysteries in a case often can be attributed to normal things through proper research. But in Peggy's case, Jayne is clear: "I just know there's something more."

Something, like what ensued in a pendulum session Jayne and her team recently conducted with Peggy, during which the pendulum "went crazy" while Jayne asked Peggy a series of questions. The next morning Jayne couldn't find the notebook she had used during the session. Finally, after searching extensively, she found it perched in the beams of her basement ceiling. "I couldn't even reach it," she recalled. "My husband had to use a ladder to get it." Jayne speculated that perhaps Peggy did not want the information gained during the pendulum session to get out.

Jayne's commitment to unraveling Peggy's mysteries is understandable. As she states on her website, her team believes the doll displays strong evidence of paranormal activity, and the case will be ongoing for some time. She also shared these thoughts with the author:

"This case, above all others, seems to leave me and my team with more questions than answers, at least at this stage. When people hear about 'haunted dolls,' images from Hollywood movies usually spring to mind and it can seem a bit lighthearted and comical. However, what we are actually dealing with here are cases of spirit attachment, and this can happen not only to dolls but other physical objects. I hope in time that this field of the paranormal receives greater understanding and consideration."

Because of the numerous reports of illness, headaches, and nightmares occurring after viewing Peggy's picture, the author suggests using discretion when looking at the image on the next page. You might want to say a blessing or prayer while you're at it. Peggy seems to have some unresolved issues, and there's no sense in needlessly becoming part of them.

Peggy

Chapter 7

Harold

"One of the most haunted dolls in the world."

– Zak Bagans, *Ghost Adventures*

Harold is famous for being the first "haunted doll" auctioned off on eBay. In 2003, the original lister, Greg, put the shabby looking composite doll up for sale along with an incredible story. He wrote that he bought Harold at a flea market from an old farmer who claimed the doll was responsible for his son's death. Greg didn't really believe the story until he experienced his own run of bad luck: he lost his cat, his girlfriend, and started suffering from chronic migraines, all within two days of purchasing the doll. He stored Harold away for a year in his basement, where he periodically heard children laughing and crying. Of course, when he went to investigate, there was no one there but Harold.

Thinking he'd maybe get $30 for the dilapidated doll, Greg couldn't believe his eyes when the bidding went all the way up to $700. Unfortunately, that bidder didn't pay, so Greg relisted and ended up selling Harold to a family friend, Kathy, for $300. By this time, news of the "eBay haunted doll" was all over the Internet and was even the topic one night on Art Bell's *Coast to Coast* show. New owner Kathy was well-aware of Harold's celebrity status and was planning to cash in herself by restoring and then reselling the doll after four months or so. She also knew something else, something Greg had told her right up front: The whole haunted story was a hoax. He was just trying to help his brother sell his antiques on eBay. (Greg revealed his secret in a blog post in October 2009.)

That should have been the end of the saga, but in reality a whole new chapter was just starting. Kathy, who was living in Ireland at the time, recalled that strange things started happening soon after she received Harold in the mail. Because of Greg's admission, she didn't connect those things to the doll at the time, and finally put it away in a closet, her plans to restore and resell it temporarily put on hold. Then, when two of her friends died inexplicably within a six-month period, and one of those friends had stayed in the same room where Harold was stored, Kathy began having second thoughts about the doll. She put Harold up for sale on eBay in 2004 and stated that she didn't believe the doll was haunted, per se. She believed it was cursed.

Author and speaker Anthony Quinata was intrigued when he saw Kathy's listing. He was looking for so-called haunted objects to test for a new book he was writing. He placed a bid on Harold but didn't even come close to the reserve Kathy had put on it. When he emailed her to ask why the reserve was so high, she told him it reflected the price she paid. She also reiterated to him that she thought

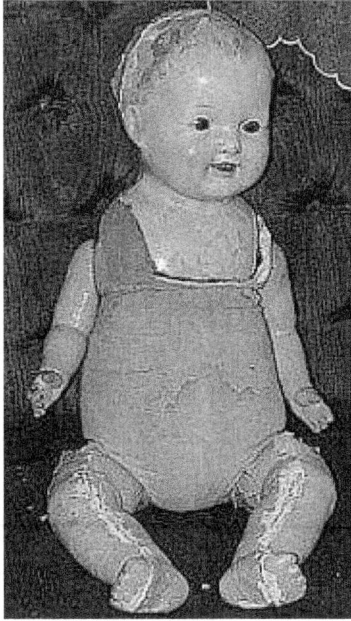

Harold

the doll was cursed and described the events that had happened to her during her time with Harold. Although he didn't plan to, Anthony soon found himself in a bidding war with someone called "Strange Majik" and ended up winning the auction for $720. Kathy immediately contacted him and offered to let him off the hook. "I'm really worried about you having this doll," she wrote. "I should have just thrown it in the ocean." Anthony insisted that a deal was a deal, and a few weeks later he received a package in the mail from Ireland.

Soon after unpacking his newly-acquired doll, Anthony subjected it to a series of tests using an EMF detector, an EVP detector, and a camera. To his disappointment, neither his instruments nor his naked eye perceived anything out-of-the-ordinary about Harold. He decided to ask his friend and colleague, psychic April Palmer, if she would do a reading of the doll. April agreed, and Anthony prepared for the session by setting up his digital voice recorder and splashing Harold with holy water as a precaution. April chuckled and placed Harold in her lap. Within two minutes, April pushed the doll away and told Anthony, "I'm sorry, but I just can't do this anymore." She said the doll had threatened to kill her, at which point she felt as if something was squeezing her heart. Anthony checked his voice recorder. At the time April was doing her reading, a voice was captured on the recorder clearly saying, "I'm going to kill you… you bitch!" A few moments later in the recording, after April was heard telling Anthony what had just happened, an evil laugh occurred.

Over the next year, many strange and terrifying things happened to Anthony and others who came in contact with Harold. Some people were physically injured; others, including Anthony, experienced horrifying visions; and Anthony himself sustained an injury that required surgery. Deeming the doll too dangerous to be out in the open, Anthony packed it away in a storage shed in 2005, where it remained until 2013.

In the fall of 2013, when a friend told him about Harold being mentioned in a YouTube video about haunted dolls, Anthony decided to come forward and set the record straight. He went public and explained that he was the current owner of Harold and had been since 2004. He also set up a website devoted to Harold on which he posts regular updates on the doll's doings, as well as reports from other people who have had Harold intrude in their lives—often in terrible ways—simply by being near him, joking about him, or looking at his photos and/or videos.

One section of the website describes the results of an investigation into Harold by Lockdown Paranormal, a non-profit paranormal group made up of retired and active law enforcement personnel. Their team conducted a three-hour testing session with Harold, and by the time they were done, they vowed to have nothing more to do with the doll ever again. One of the team members claimed to have heard frightening EVPs, after which he experienced a migraine, severe disorientation, and then the horrible sensation of being hit in the head with a baseball bat. Next, his back went out and he fell to the floor, unable to move for hours. The investigators concluded that there may be a malevolent entity attached to Harold, and that it would be safer for everyone if they conducted no further investigation.

In 2014, the crew from *Ghost Adventures* took Harold with them to Mexico, where they were preparing to do a show about the infamous Island of the Dolls in Xochimilco. Before they left for the island, the crew asked a highly-regarded psychic medium, known as Sabrinah, to "read" the doll. Sabrinah told them through an interpreter that there were five different spirits in Harold, and that they needed to treat the doll well or the spirits would get angry and "attack." She further specified that if they did something wrong, and angered one of the spirits, "you guys could get broken hands." At first that warning didn't make a lot of sense to the crew, but minutes later it became clearer. While getting in the car after the session with Sabrinah, lead investigator Zak Bagans felt a sharp pain on his upper left arm. When he looked he saw three little bruises that seemingly appeared out of nowhere. They matched perfectly the fingers on Harold's hand. Zak suddenly remembered that Harold's left arm and hand were severely damaged and needed to be treated very gently. Was this a not-so-subtle message to Zak, the only person who had handled Harold on the trip?

There are many questions surrounding Harold, many of which will likely stay unanswered. Anthony Quinata is determined to answer as many as he can, no matter how long it takes. "What is the truth behind what is going on with this doll?" That's the question Anthony poses on his Harold the Haunted Doll website. Viewers are asked to join him on his journey to find answers.

Then again, you might want to think about that first.

Chapter 8

Lingering Spirits

The following dolls may not have as much media documentation and witness corroboration attached to them as our previous little fiends, er, friends, but their stories are still good for plenty of goosebumps. The legends and lore attached to some of these dolls have been around longer than most of us. It could be that as time went on, legends expanded, tales grew taller, and fact and fiction took on slightly new meanings. Alternatively, it could be that the stories are, for the most part, true. Most legends, after all, do begin with a kernel of truth. The reader is asked to look at these accounts as the dolls' owners once looked at their precious playthings: with childlike wonder and openness.

Pupa

Pupa is a 14-inch tall felt doll whose first known home was Trieste, Italy, in the 1920s. She was given to a little girl who adored the doll so much that she kept it in her possession throughout her adult years right up to her death in 2005. According to the woman's grandchildren, the woman believed that Pupa was alive. Not only did the doll move on its own and talk to her, she claimed, but it was her best friend and even saved her life once.

Pupa never left the woman's side all those years. It traveled with her from Italy to the United States, back to Italy, across Europe, and eventually back to America again, where it currently is housed.

The family that owns the doll now (they wish for their identity to remain private) takes great pains to protect Pupa by keeping her in a glass case. She still wears her original blue felt suit, and her hair, which is made of human hair, is as resplendent as ever. Pupa reportedly is as active as ever, too. Family members claim that the doll is often found in different positions from where she was left, that other objects in the case with her get pushed around, and that tapping is sometimes heard coming from inside the case, followed by the sight of the doll's hand pressed up against the glass. There are also reports that on several occasions the case has steamed up and the words "Pupa hate" have been inscribed in a child-like scrawl on the inside of the glass.

Several years ago, a member of the family reported that he actually videotaped the doll getting up and walking inside the case. He tried to post the video on YouTube, but all three attempts resulted in footage of nothing but a mysterious white film overlaid with the words "Pupa No!" appearing in child-like writing.

Pupa's new family speculates that the well-traveled doll misses her original owner and wants desperately to get out of her enclosed environment and be reunited with her long-time companion.

Joliet

According to Joliet's current owner, Anna, Joliet is not just a beat-up-looking antique doll from a bygone era, but a vessel of precious, innocent souls. Whose souls? Those of four baby boys, Anna's son included. As the story goes, Joliet was cursed generations ago by a bitter woman, who, moved by jealousy, gave the doll to Anna's great-grandmother as a pregnancy gift. Great Grandma soon gave birth to a beautiful baby boy, only to experience the heartbreak of losing him three days later to a sudden illness. Soon after this tragedy, the mother started hearing a baby's cries in the middle of the night, and discovered they were coming from Joliet. As distressing as this was, she had no doubt the cries were those of her son, and believing he was somehow trapped inside the doll, she could not bear to get rid of it for fear of losing her son completely.

Joliet was passed down to Anna's grandmother, who knew about her brother's death as an infant and the belief by her mother that his soul was trapped inside the doll. But when her own baby boy died unexpectedly at three days old, it became apparent to the family that this wasn't a mere coincidence. It was a curse. Like her mother, Anna's grandmother also heard crying coming from Joliet, but now it was *two* distinct cries.

Anna's mother experienced the curse in the exact same way. She had two children, a boy and a girl. The boy died on the third day of his life. When the doll was passed down to her, Anna accepted it with a heavy heart. She knew the fate that awaited her, but she also accepted that she was now the caretaker of the little souls inside Joliet. She could bring no harm to the doll. Sadly, the morbid script of the curse played itself out in Anna's life as well. Her son added a fourth voice to the cacophony of cries that she hears each night coming from Joliet. It is terrible yet morbidly reassuring to know the babies are in some way still with her. The worst part is watching her daughter at play and knowing that someday Joliet will belong to her and that the curse will continue.

Emilia

Emilia is a doll that is as old as she looks. She was a gift from King Umberto of Italy (who reigned from 1878-1900) to a bright and cheerful little girl named Marie, who was the daughter of the Captain of the Royal Guard .

From the start, Marie and Emilia were inseparable. Marie shared her secrets with Emilia and hugged the doll tight when hiding in shelters during the world wars. Marie claimed that Emilia would frequently blink at her and move her arms around on her own. A man sitting next to them in a shelter one day said Emilia smiled at him.

During World War II, Marie (and Emilia, of course) were on a train headed to Udine, Italy, when a bomb went off inside the train. Marie narrowly escaped unscathed, but Emilia was not so lucky. Both of the doll's arms and scalp were blown off in the explosion, and she looked like something a junk yard dog wouldn't even bother with. But Marie would not part with her beloved companion. Not only was the doll a gift from the king, but a woman traveling with Marie died in the explosion while trying to retrieve the doll. Marie would never forget that.

In the years that followed, it seemed the doll never forgot either. People reported seeing sadness in Emilia's eyes and facial expressions. At night, Marie heard weeping and crying coming from the doll. At times it cried for its mama. Once it spoke words to Marie, but Marie couldn't understand them. Because all of this was happening after the explosion—the explosion that shattered the doll's voice box—Marie had no doubt that the doll now was haunted by the soul of the woman who died on the train.

Years after the war ended, Marie had a daughter and named her Emilia. Her daughter takes care of the doll now, and she too claims to hear noises coming from it. Sad noises from a sad doll.

Okiku

In 1918, 17-year-old Eikichi Suzuki took a trip to the town of Sapporo, located on the Japanese island of Hokkaido, for a marine exhibition. While strolling along the city's famous shopping street, Tanuki-koji, he spotted a doll in a store window that he knew his little two-year-old sister, Okiku, would love. The female doll, dressed in a traditional Japanese kimono, was about 40 cm tall, with black piercing eyes made of beads, a flesh-colored face, and black hair about shoulder length. He bought it for her immediately and his instincts were proven correct as soon as he returned home. Okiku played with the doll day and night and even named it after herself. They were as inseparable as sisters.

But tragedy struck a year later, when Okiku died after contracting a serious cold. (Some researchers believe the little girl may actually have died of the Spanish flu.) To keep Okiku's memory alive, her parents set her beloved doll in a place of honor on the family altar. After some time had passed, the family noticed something strange about the doll—its hair had grown noticeably longer, and the ends, which before were neat and evenly cut, were now a bit more frayed and haphazard in length. The astounded family continued to watch over the ensuing months as the doll's hair eventually grew down to its knees. This was proof, they believed, that Okiku's restless spirit had somehow taken refuge in the doll, a belief that was comforting and troubling at the same time.

In 1938, the Suzuki family moved to Sakhalin, but decided not to take the peculiar doll with them. They had no intention of simply discarding it, as they firmly believed it contained their daughter's spirit, so they brought the doll to the Mannenji temple in the town of Iwamizawa, Hokkaido. The priest there listened patiently as the Suzukis explained how the doll's hair grew on its own, even after it was cut repeatedly, as they had been doing. It didn't take long before the priest witnessed this phenomenon himself, and soon trimming the doll's hair became a ritual event at the temple.

It has since been determined that the doll's hair is indeed human, although this in itself is not too surprising, as that was a common feature of dolls of that time. Some skeptics think the Okiku doll is an example of a "clockwork doll" and contains a mechanism inside of it that slowly extends the hair over time. The hair is rewound to affect the look of a new haircut. That explanation, though, has never been proven and would require the duplicity of a great number of people, including the Suzuki family and the priests and monks of the Mannenji temple.

Whatever force is behind the mysterious Okiku doll, be it natural or supernatural, it has created a mystery that has lasted for decades and shows no signs of stopping. Visitors are always welcome at Okiku's home at the Mannenji temple, where she is displayed in a modest wooden case. Her beady black eyes have been described as pools of unfathomable depths. Perhaps if you gazed into them long enough, she would tell you the real story herself.

Okiku in the Mannenji Temple

Chapter 9

Island of the Dolls

If one doll is creepy, then hundreds of them—decayed, mutilated, and hanging from trees—has got to register at least as "freaky" on the weirdness scale. "Terrifying" if you were to be trapped with them at night.

This isn't a retelling of someone's bad dream. It is the actual description of a place in Mexico called Isla de las Munecas, the Island of the Dolls. Located just south of Mexico City amidst the canals of Xochimilco, this small uninhabited man-made island has become one of the strangest tourist attractions ever. Even though it entails a two-hour boat ride to get there, tourists and locals alike make the journey regularly not only to view the gruesome display, but also to pay homage to the spirits that are said to haunt the island.

Island of the Dolls

The story behind Isla de las Munecas began in 1950 with a zealous man named Don Julian Santana Barrera. At around this time, Don Julian took it upon himself to boisterously proclaim Christianity in the streets. But not only did his preaching fall on deaf ears, it put him in harm's way, as there were many who felt he had no business proclaiming religion in public and who had no compunction about beating him up to get their point across.

Facing hostility and rejection, and struggling with alcoholism, Don Julian left his wife and children and took refuge on a small garden island where he would live as the sole occupant and caretaker for the next 50 years. According to legend, shortly after arriving on the island, Don Julian discovered the body of a little girl who had drowned in the canal. He also found a doll, presumably hers, floating nearby, which he retrieved and hung in a tree as a sign of respect toward the girl's spirit and to protect the island from any further evil.

But one doll apparently wasn't enough. Distraught that he had not been able to somehow save the little girl, and wanting to make her happy in the afterlife, Don Julian began collecting more dolls. He fished discarded dolls from the canals, and on his rare trips into town, he rummaged through trash bins in search of more. Sometimes he traded his home-grown fruits and vegetables for dolls. He didn't care what their condition was like—headless, limbless, sun-bleached, burnt—he took any and all and hung them up wherever there was an available tree limb or fence post. He even built a little wooden shed where he housed his most special dolls, attending to it like a shrine.

The doll shed

Rumors about Don Julian grew, of course, as much as his macabre doll collection did. Some people said he was insane and that he believed his dolls were real children. Others reported hearing him say that the dolls came alive at night and walked around the island. Knowledge of Don Julian's bizarre island retreat was for decades limited to the local residents, but that changed in the early 1990s when work was done to clear the canals of excessive water lilies. Word soon got out about the hermit living in a hut on an island with hundreds of creepy dolls.

A small but steady stream of visitors, reporters, and even political figures began venturing to the island via trajineras, or Mexican gondolas, and Don Julian welcomed them graciously. He explained that he believed the dolls kept away evil spirits and that they helped his garden grow. He also believed the island was haunted by the spirit of the little girl who drowned in the canal. And for reasons that only made sense to him, he believed that by displaying hundreds of discarded dolls in the island's trees, he could make that little girl's spirit happy.

In April 2001, Don Julian's nephew, Anastasio, came out to the island to visit his uncle and help him plant pumpkins. The two took a fishing break on the morning of April 21st, and before long Don Julian started singing. He told his nephew that he was singing to appease the mermaids, who were trying to entice him into the water. Anastasio had heard his uncle ramble on about mermaids before, so not being particularly concerned, he left him for about an hour to begin the pumpkin planting. When he returned, he found his uncle face down in the canal. Don Julian died in the same water as the little girl he had been devoted to all those years.

The official cause of Don Julian's death was listed as a heart attack, which it is believed had caused him to fall into the canal. Since that time, the island has become an even bigger tourist attraction, and has been featured in numerous articles and television shows. When *Ghost Adventures* filmed an episode about the island in 2014, the crew experienced a number of unexplained phenomena, including a fire starting by itself, shadowy figures outside and inside the hut, cans moving, a distant scream, and most disturbingly, repeated laughter from a doll too old to have a working voice box.

Don Julian's family takes care of the island now and it is open for visitors on weekends. Not much has been done to change the original design. The same dirty, moldy, broken, cobweb-strewn and insect-infested dolls hang where they have hung for decades. Some who make the journey bring dolls of their own to leave as an offering to the spirits. Candles, candies, and coins are other common gifts that are left. Many visitors have reported hearing ghostly whispers while walking among the dolls. Don Julian's nephew has stated that he has seen some of the dolls move their heads and limbs. There is one doll, he said, that cries out loud.

If you suffer from pediophobia (fear of dolls), Mexico's Island of the Dolls undoubtedly will rank dead last on your list of travel destinations. But for those thrill-seekers out there and travelers who like to explore off the beaten path, you might just want to book the next available *trajinera*.

And don't forget to bring a doll.

Chapter 10

Send in the Clowns (Or Maybe Not)

No book on haunted dolls would be complete without a chapter on creepy clown dolls. Sure, on the outside they look all happy and full of fun, but what really lurks behind those painted-on faces and big rubber noses? In the stories that follow, that answer may be not so much Bozo as Beelzebub. So if you suffer from coulrophobia (fear of clowns), you may want to read the rest of this with the lights on. If you suffer from pediophobia (fear of dolls), congratulations on reading this far. If you suffer from both, well, good luck with that.

The Restless Clown

When Thomas put his clown doll up for sale on eBay, he couldn't help but have a few mixed feelings about it. He himself was a doll sculptor, and he originally bought the doll because with his trained eye he saw a lot of character in its face. What he soon found out was that in addition to character, the doll contained a whole lot of something—or *someone*—else. As he explained in his auction listing: "Ever since I had this clown doll, weird things started to happen." Those weird things included the sounds of children giggling and whispering, as well as footsteps in empty spaces. But the most unsettling thing about the doll was that it seemed to move by itself.

The first time that Thomas left the doll in one place and came back to find it somewhere else, he chalked it up to his imagination. The second time, he started to doubt his memory. Did he actually put the clown where he thought he had? So to prove to himself what was really going on, he set the doll in a corner of his living room, made a note of where it was exactly, and left it there for three days. When he returned, the clown had moved about three feet from its original position.

At this point, Thomas was eager to find out more about the doll's origins, so he contacted the man who sold it to him. The man told him that he had bought the doll from an antique shop. Thomas asked him if he had noticed anything strange about the doll during the time he owned it. "Yes!" replied the man without hesitation. "It moves!" The man went on to say that his wife made him put the doll in the shed, as she was so freaked out by it.

Thomas felt a little better that he wasn't the only one who had experienced surreal events around the doll. But now the question remained, what to do with it? As much as he admired the doll for its craftsmanship and unique look, he had to admit to himself that he wasn't comfortable with it in his home. So he did what a lot of people in the digital age do with haunted objects: he put it up for sale on eBay.

Rachel wasn't planning on buying a haunted doll that day, but fate apparently had other plans. She had been reading ghost stories on the Web when she entered the word "haunted" in a search engine. An eBay auction came up in the results, and it only had four minutes to go. Rachel clicked on it and read with growing fascination the account of the "haunted clown doll." She was equally amazed that the bidding was currently in the hundreds.

Having grown up with friends who lived in an old haunted house in a small town in Washington, Rachel had developed an early interest in the paranormal. She had to admit, it would be pretty cool to own a genuine haunted doll. The more she stared at the photo of the unusual-looking clown doll, the more she felt a crazy compulsion struggling to surface. Surface it did, and Rachel entered a bid. A few moments later she received notification that she had won the auction for about five hundred dollars.

Rachel suddenly felt nervous. Did she really want that doll to come straight to the house? Thinking, *maybe not right away*, she obtained a post office box and asked Thomas to send the doll there. When her package arrived several days later, Rachel opened it tentatively, but soon relaxed when the straw-stuffed doll with the big rubber head and round nose showed no interest in jumping out and attacking her or chatting her up in a deep, diabolical voice. She brought it home and named it Vincent Hitchcock, after the two legendary icons of horror cinema, Vincent Price and Alfred Hitchcock.

When Rachel first brought Vincent home, she placed him in a corner of a spare bedroom. Nothing strange happened in the days that followed, and Rachel started to wonder if maybe she had bought just an ordinary old doll. Then one day several weeks later she walked into the bedroom to grab a laundry basket and was greeted by an unexpected sight. Propped up in front of the basket was Vincent, staring at Rachel with wide eyes as if he had been expecting her. Her first reaction was to accuse her boyfriend and teenage daughter of moving the doll, but they both vehemently denied it. With no other explanation, Rachel was a little spooked, but also, secretly, a little thrilled. Perhaps the doll *was* haunted. Isn't that what she wanted?

Eager now to monitor the doll's activities, Rachel took Vincent out of the spare bedroom and gave him his own "place of honor" in a more visible part of the house where the whole family could keep on eye on him. According to Rachel, Vincent moved on his own several more times since that first incident. And once the family found him with his arm sticking straight up in the air.

Vincent showed another side of himself during multiple sessions when Rachel left audio recording equipment beside him in an otherwise empty room. The captured EVPs, which for a while Rachel had available on her now-defunct website, revealed a gravelly male voice saying on separate occasions: "Get rid of it," "Run," and either "I love you" or "I left you." But the most disturbing and clearest EVP was a loud command: "Wake up!" When Rachel's daughter heard the playback, she turned white and told her mother she had been awakened by that very voice the previous night.

As of this writing, it is unknown if Vincent is still with Rachel. It is likely he is, as Rachel told one journalist that she feels Vincent has a childlike aura around him that suggests a child's spirit resides in him, or a spirit with a childlike nature. It's nothing to be afraid of. And if he occasionally takes an unexpected stroll around the house? It's just something you get used to.

The Spooky Couch Clown

Unlike Rachel in our previous story, Becky Smith would never welcome a clown of any kind into her home. It's not that she fears the supernatural; she's a psychic sensitive and has experienced many strange phenomena in her life. But she does fear clowns to an excessive degree. For over twenty years she had been harboring a frightening memory that she finally told to the readers of *True Ghost Tales* in 2010. Relating her story was therapeutic in one sense—and terrifying in another. Her story goes like this:

When Becky was in her early teens, she and her sister, brother, and mom spent several months living with her grandparents in New Mexico while her father was away in the military. One day her mom's brother and his wife,

Debby, arrived for a week-long visit. Debby was eager to show the girls the present she had just received from their Uncle Robert: a clown doll.

Not only did Becky not share her aunt's love of dolls, she also had a fear of clowns. So needless to say, this new house guest didn't impress her much. Plus, it had such realistic blue eyes that it unnerved her to look at it for too long. The doll's painted face was made of porcelain, as were its hands and feet. Only six inches tall, it sat with its legs stretched out while holding a small jack-in-the-box in its lap. After making the expected polite conversation about the doll, Becky went to bed and thought nothing more of it.

The next day when Becky and her sister arrived home from school, the first thing they saw was the doll, staring at them as they came through the door. Apparently, Aunt Debby had placed it on the sofa before she and Uncle Robert went out for the day. The clown seemed to have an expectant look on its face, as if it was waiting for someone. The sisters gave each other a "whatever" look and ran to their room to change out of their school clothes. But first, Becky turned the doll face down into the pile of pillows on the sofa. She really didn't like that clown watching her.

Having changed their clothes, the girls sauntered back into the living room and pulled up short. The clown was sitting upright on the sofa again, this time facing the hallway from which they just came. The only other person in the house was their grandmother, and they knew that she was still in her room in the back of the house. Becky turned to her sister and said, "I don't like this thing." Her sister could only nod in agreement. Becky grabbed the doll, intending to push it back into the sofa pillows, and nearly dropped it when she felt how cold it was. It was like it had just been taken out of a freezer and was frozen solid.

For the next few days, the doll seemed to follow the girls. Or maybe it would be better to say it anticipated where they were going to be—and got there first. No matter what room they went in—their bedroom, the living room, dining room, kitchen—it was there with its expectant eyes and knowing smile. One day Becky even found it on top of the piano when it was time for her practice. Thinking her brother was behind the doll antics, Becky complained to her mother, but when pressed, her brother swore he hadn't even seen the doll.

Becky's aunt was surprisingly nonchalant about the reports of her clown doll moving around on its own. There were a lot of people and pets (dogs) living under one roof, she offered as an explanation. Obviously her little doll was getting moved by someone, either two-footed or four. Becky wouldn't let it drop, though. She begged her aunt to pack the doll away for the duration of her stay, using her well-known clown phobia as motivation. Debby agreed and zipped the doll up in a suitcase as Becky watched. Becky's relief was immediate and palpable. Unfortunately, it wouldn't last for long.

That night Becky woke at around 2 a.m. She was thirsty and got up to get a drink of water from the kitchen. Because her grandma was afraid of the dark and used plenty of nightlights, the house wasn't completely dark. Becky passed the doorway of the front room and then suddenly stopped in amazement. At first she wasn't sure what she was seeing, thinking perhaps weird shadows from the dim lighting was causing tricks on her eyes. For there in front of her, sitting upright on the sofa as if it was the most natural thing in the world, was the clown. She tentatively took a step forward and was shocked further awake by the bone-chilling cold that filled the room. And then the impossible happened: the clown rolled his eyes sideways to look right at Becky. Then he followed with his head.

Becky wanted to scream but was physically unable to muster a sound. All she could do was reach deep down to her Baptist roots and pray. Believing the doll contained an evil spirit, she somehow found her voice and commanded whatever was in the clown doll to leave. Then she walked over to the sofa, acting braver than she felt, and switched on a lamp. As light washed over the clown's face, Becky watched incredulously as it opened its mouth into a toothy grin and shook its head back and forth like it was telling her "no." Becky remembered losing track of time as she and the doll stared at each other in the most insane game ever of "don't blink."

Finally Becky broke contact and rubbed her eyes. She opened and closed them several times over, hoping each time that the ghastly scene before her would vanish and that she was simply in the middle of a sleepwalking nightmare. But each time she opened her eyes, the clown was still there, piercing her with its icy blue stare. It's only a dream, she thought. It has to be. She forced herself to continue to the kitchen for her glass of water. Then she dashed back through the front room without once looking at the sofa.

The next morning when she awoke, the first thing Becky saw was the glass of water sitting on her nightstand. She knew then, with a sense of dread, that the events of the previous night had not been a dream. She beelined to the living room, and sure enough, there was the doll, still sitting on the sofa and still bathed in the light from the lamp Becky had turned on just hours earlier. It wasn't grinning with an open mouth anymore, but its head was turned toward Becky's bedroom, as if it had watched her go back to bed.

Because no one had believed her or her sister in the past about the doll, Becky didn't tell any of the adults about what had happened. Uncle Robert and Aunt Debby left a couple of days later, taking their creepy little companion with them. To this day, some twenty years later, Becky and her sister still get uncomfortable talking about that week with the doll. Interestingly, she has heard from various family members through the years that no matter where her uncle and aunt moved to, the clown always ended up on the couch.

The Nightmare Clowns

Sarah loved her collection of clown dolls. So much so that she had an entire room set aside in her house just for them. A devotee of clowns ever since her first trip to the circus as a child, Sarah had amassed dozens of dolls of every shape and size imaginable. Some were obvious collector's editions, while others were simply old children's toys. Most had happy facial expressions and a few had sad or surprised faces. They were all delightful in their own way.

All except for the two newest ones. The two that moved around on their own.

Sarah had bought these two clown dolls—a boy and a girl—from an antiques dealer about two months earlier. They were part of a five-doll limited edition set. Sarah couldn't believe her luck and was ecstatic about adding them to her collection. When she brought them home, she placed them on a bookcase shelf in a space dedicated just for them. They looked great there amongst all the other clowns, Sarah thought with satisfaction. But why is the house suddenly so cold?

The chill in the house continued unabated, which Sarah couldn't figure out since it had always been warm, bright, and cheerful. Then a few days later, other odd things started occurring. Sarah heard rustling noises, like something moving around, that she couldn't attribute to any source. At night in bed, she heard tapping within the walls. It would start in one spot and then make its way all around the room. Lights would turn on and off by themselves. But most upsetting was when she walked into her doll room and discovered that her two newest clown dolls weren't where they were supposed to be.

The first couple of times this happened, Sarah assumed she absent-mindedly moved them after cleaning. The rational part of her mind told her it had to be her; after all, no one else lived in the house. But then she started having nightmares in which she was being chased by shadowy monsters that morphed into evil-looking, leering clowns with bright red lips that parted to show rows of sharp and pointy teeth. The nightmares increased in frequency until she was having them every night.

The nightmares weren't the only things increasing in frequency. So did the strange sounds, the on-and-off-lights, and the dolls moving around by themselves. It reached a crescendo when one night Sarah awoke from a particularly intense nightmare and couldn't shake the feeling of there being an abnormal energy in the air. She got up and tentatively walked down the hall to the small study that housed her dolls. She knew before turning on the light what she would see, and sure enough, she was right: the two new dolls had moved again. This time the boy clown lay in a corner of the room, far removed from his original perch. The other, the girl clown, was reclining on top of the heads of two other dolls. Sarah felt sick to her stomach and resolved at that instant that she would seek help the next day.

The help Sarah sought, and received, came from paranormal investigator and demonologist John Zaffis. And the account of Sarah and her scary clown dolls is told in more detail in Zaffis' book *Haunted by the Things You Love*. Sarah had gotten John's name from an acquaintance, and after calling him in the morning, she was able to set up an appointment with him for that evening.

When John arrived at Sarah's house, he listened as she explained everything that had been happening since bringing the two clown dolls home. Then he examined the dolls himself. John could tell from his many years of experience that the dolls did indeed have a spirit problem. Another clue was the dark shadow he saw out of the corner of his eye slithering quickly across the room when he picked up the dolls. He assured Sarah that something could be done about the dolls, but he first wanted to talk to the antique dealer Sarah had bought them from. The more information he had, the better. He left, but not before putting the dolls in the garage.

John found out from the shop owner that the other three dolls in the set had been purchased in the time since Sarah bought hers. Two of the dolls went to one woman, and the third doll to someone else. The owner refused to give John their names, or the name of the original owner. She did add, though, that she hated having those dolls in the shop and would never take in any clowns again. They gave her an uneasy, "creepy" feeling.

His suspicions about the dolls having been confirmed, John returned to Sarah's house the next day to take care of the two little pests. He was glad to hear, but not surprised, that Sarah had not had any trouble since putting the clowns in the garage. The atmosphere in the house had changed, too, she said. It was back to normal: quiet and peaceful. John then explained that spirit energy had definitely attached itself to her dolls. It could have come from the strong emotional attachment the previous owner had toward them, or it could be that a "wandering" spirit attached itself to the dolls and started "acting up" when the circumstances were right. In this case, being added to Sarah's collection perhaps activated the spirit, and it grew stronger and more troublesome as it fed off the fear Sarah increasingly projected.

Though John was confident that no spirit had attached itself to Sarah, he still advised her to have a minister or spiritual person bless and cleanse the house to take care of any residual energy that could be lingering. As for the clowns, John took them back to his home, performed cleansing and binding rituals over them, and eventually placed them in his Museum of the Paranormal, where they keep company with the many other "problem" dolls John has confiscated over the years while working in the paranormal realm.

If that was the end of the story, it would be quite enough to keep any sane person from purchasing an antique clown doll. But there is more. Soon after John took care of Sarah's dolls, he received a call from the woman who had bought two of the other clowns from the same shop. Rhonda told John she had also been experiencing strange events since purchasing the dolls, but her account was even more terrifying than Sarah's. In addition to horrific nightmares, she was seeing shadows flit about her house, having objects knocked over, and hearing inexplicable noises at all hours. But it was the dolls themselves that were sending her into a panic. They didn't just limit their movements to one room like Sarah's—they moved all over the house! Rhonda would come home to find one in her pantry, one in her bathroom . . . one even propped up on her bed. She tried throwing them in the trash, but somehow they made their way back into the house. At that point, Rhonda was too afraid to try anything else with them, so she contacted John.

John came over as soon as he could and performed a cleansing and binding ritual on the dolls right there on Rhonda's property. He was preparing to take them to the museum when Rhonda did an unexpected about-face and said she wanted the dolls back. After all, they were okay now, right? No more ghosts or goblins to contend with? John tried to warn her that it wasn't a good idea to keep them. The binding could be compromised if they were handled or disturbed in any way. Rhonda wouldn't budge, though. She'd keep the dolls safe, she assured him. And that was that. John has not heard back from her as of this writing.

As for the last clown doll from the antique shop? The buyer of that doll also contacted John, telling him she felt there was an "evil presence" attached to it. She constantly saw shadows moving about the house, and heard strange tapping noises within the walls. John made an appointment to see her, but before that day arrived, a package came to his door. It was the fifth clown doll with a note attached that in no uncertain terms made it clear the owner wanted nothing to do with that doll ever again. She didn't even want John to come to the house in fear of him "stirring things up."

After dealing with all of the clown dolls from the antique shop, John now believes that the entire collection had been used in an occult ritual, and that spirits had been summoned to lodge in the dolls. For what purpose remains a mystery.

Chapter 11

Buyer Beware: The Haunted Doll Trade

As we've seen, you don't have to wait to find your very own demonic doll hiding in the attic or until the eccentric neighbor down the block gives you her 100-year-old Baby Betsy, who, by the way, likes to play hide-and-seek at night . . . and who teases she's going to kill you . . . but it's so cute the way she says it!

Nope, now you can just go online and buy a possessed/haunted/cursed/spirit-attached little plaything any time the mood strikes (which hopefully is only after ingesting copious amounts of alcohol). Just move your cursor to the eBay icon on your computer and if you're lucky, you might be able to snag a Haunted Hank doll for a devilishly good price, free shipping included.

Once bastions of such innocent fare as baseball cards, cheap electronics, and homemade Christmas ornaments, major buying and selling sites like eBay and Etsy have revealed in recent years that they have darker corridors for those customers with *unique* interests. In August 2013, there were multiple bidders for an eBay doll described as: "Nasty Perverse Possessed Doll!" It sold for $1,526. More recently, a doll named Valora went for $285. This doll was described as containing the spirit of a powerful (good) witch who grants wishes, bring blessings, heals pets, and is good with kids.

Not all haunted dolls come with a hefty price tag, though. At the time of this writing, there were 188 haunted dolls listed on eBay, and the vast majority of them were priced less than $100.

Over at Etsy, Nancy Oyola runs Nancy's Haunted Doll Shop. She says that her psychic grandmother left her with more than 300 haunted dolls when she died. Nancy has been selling them online for several years and has amassed a loyal customer following. Judging from the abundance of positive reviews on her site, it seems that buyers are indeed receiving more than just a physical doll, and are quite happy about it:

"This Doll has a very strong energy from the moment I took her out the box."

"He started sparkling to let me know his spirit is very much present and active!"

"I suspect he may have tried to read some of the books on which he was seated yesterday because they were all mysteriously toppled down on the floor with him sitting next to them! What a character!"

"The eyes DO follow everywhere and I almost feel like there is a 'real' person here."

"I felt her positive energy right away. I'm sure she will be a treasured member of my spirit doll family!"

"Spirit dolls" is what haunted doll collectors commonly call their prized possessions. They typically believe that a lost soul has taken refuge in an earthly vessel that, in this case, is a doll. Many vendors claim to be psychics themselves, or know psychics or mediums who have communicated with these spirits, thus enabling them to include a complete background story with each doll they list for sale.

Some dealers refuse to refer to their transactions as sales, insisting instead that they facilitate "adoptions." Paranormal investigator and haunted doll trader Jayne Harris, whom we met in Chapter 6 ("Peggy"), is one such dealer who takes her work very seriously. "I don't give them out to just anybody," she told reporter Jak Hutchcraft in a Vice.com article. Some people want a haunted doll because they either can't have children of their own or they've lost a child tragically. Other people are simply looking for companionship. Still others want the thrill of a paranormal experience. Jayne takes extreme care to match up a doll with a new owner or family, and takes into account many factors when deciding whether or not to go through with an adoption. Someone looking for a "replacement child," for example, may not be the best candidate, as bringing an active spirit into their life may only wreak havoc with their emotional vulnerability.

The owner of over 20 haunted dolls, collector Katrin Reedik offers another line of reasoning as to why someone may want a haunted doll. In an interview with the *UK Daily Mail*, Reedik said: "Why not? If you have an interest in the paranormal then you can always start with dolls. They don't need so much of your time and effort. But remember—they need to be respected. They were once living people just like us . . . They can be companions, friends and teachers. They can teach you a lot about death, afterlife and more. One day you may discover your mediumistic skills as a result of connecting with spirit dolls."

Most, if not all dealers, are emphatic that their dolls "are of the positive white light," and not to be feared. But as we all know, in life, and apparently in death, there are no guarantees. It does happen every so often that someone buying a spirit doll will obtain Demonic Dan instead of Angelic Ann. Or maybe the doll's not outright evil, but is just more "active" than the buyer anticipated. While some people might be delighted with that outcome, others might be looking for the nearest sage stick or exorcist.

The very first eBay "haunted doll," Harold, was given his own extensive coverage in Chapter 7. Here are a few other auction dolls who have reportedly given their owners a bit more than bargained for.

Amanda

Amanda is a bisque-headed doll believed to have been created by German doll maker Heinrich Handwerck in the late 1800s. Amanda first appeared on eBay in 2003. Later that year, she was put back on eBay by her new owner, who claimed the doll was making strange things happen. Since then, Amanda has been auctioned off many times over, with each consecutive owner claiming basically the same thing: the doll caused havoc in their life.

One woman wrote that she became obsessed with Amanda and could not stop thinking about her. It got to the point where she believed she and the doll were sharing thoughts telepathically. Amanda invaded her dreams as well. One night, the woman had the horrifying feeling that she was being "dragged" into Amanda's dream. She woke with freezing feet and was shocked to see that they were blue and covered with scratches. She started to call an ambulance when suddenly her feet appeared normal again. She looked at Amanda, who was perched nearby, and swore the doll flashed her a devilish grin.

Other past owners have claimed that Amanda moved on her own, broke objects in their home, and brought bad luck into their lives. The doll now resides with paranormal investigators in Atlanta, Georgia, where she is often heard to scratch on the glass case in which she is housed.

Bebé

Bebé is a beautiful red-haired doll from the mid-1970s. A few years ago, she became part of a family of 25 haunted dolls when collector Janice Poole purchased her off of eBay. Janice, a paranormal investigator as well as doll collector, admitted that her southern California home was perfectly normal until the dolls moved in. Then all sorts of strange phenomena started happening. But of all her dolls, said Janice, Bebé is the most haunted of all.

As soon as Janice brought Bebé into her house, the atmosphere changed and the strange activity intensified. Janice increasingly felt like she was being watched. Doors would slam on their own; windows would fuse shut; giggling could be heard coming from empty rooms; and objects like keys would be displaced. One night Janice felt something run past her feet, but couldn't see what it was. She decided at that point to have her house blessed.

The blessing calmed things down for a little while, but then after a couple of months the disturbances resumed in full force. One night Janice heard a thumping sound coming from the attic. When she went up to investigate, she fell into a dream-like state and had a vision of a tall man entering a room and whispering angrily to someone inside. The screaming of a little girl was heard next, followed by an abrupt silence. The vision cut to inside the room, where the lifeless body of the girl was shown lying on the floor, a red-haired doll clutched in her hand. At that point, Janice suddenly woke up and was terrified to see something race past her out of the corner of her eye. When she turned her head, she saw Bebé—the same doll that was in her dream.

Janice is now convinced that her "dream" told the story of a little girl's murder, and that the girl herself haunts the doll Bebé. She is determined, with the doll's help, to find out what really happened and perhaps bring peace to a very troubled soul.

The Voodoo Doll

In 2004, a woman in Galveston, Texas, bought a genuine New Orleans Voodoo doll on eBay. The doll was described as being haunted, very active, and "almost alive," and carried the warning that it should remain bound and tied in its little metal coffin. But because the woman was interested in investigating the paranormal activities of the doll for a book she was writing, she bypassed this admonition and took the doll out for display. She immediately regretted that decision.

The doll attacked her, repeatedly, leaving visible cuts and bruises on her legs and ankles. Certain beyond all doubt that the doll was indeed *haunted*—if that was even the right word—the woman put it back in its box. But then the doll attacked her in her dreams and left her exhausted from night after night of horrible nightmares. She tried to burn it, but it wouldn't burn. She tried to cut it up, but her knife and scissors broke in the attempt. Finally, she buried it in a cemetery, but apparently not deep enough, as the next day it appeared on her front step, a bit dirty but otherwise no worse for the wear.

Fearing she was running out of options, the woman put the doll back up on eBay. It sold and she shipped it off immediately. Not long afterwards, the buyer contacted her and said the doll had disappeared. Suspecting the worst, the woman looked out her front door and, sure enough, the doll was back. She mailed it again to the buyer, who this time told her he received nothing but an empty box. For the third time, the doll found its way back to the woman's home, appearing yet again on her front step.

At this point the woman tried contacting the eBay seller from whom she obtained the doll. Her emails went unanswered. She then tried shipping it back to the seller in New Orleans. The package was returned to her with a notice attached that the resident of that address was deceased. She reached out to local paranormal groups, but they either told her they couldn't help her or didn't get back to her at all. Finally, on Halloween in 2006, she managed to tell her story on a local radio show. Several callers to the show suggested that the woman seek out a priest for help.

The woman did call a priest, who came out and blessed the antique silver box containing the doll. He also said a binding prayer to keep the spirit locked up safely inside the box. These actions seemed to work, and the doll was subsequently tucked away deep in the woman's attic with no further report of trouble.

Two years later, in 2008, the woman gave the doll to Lisa Lee Harp Waugh, a Houston area paranormal investigator, professional necromancer, and voodoo practitioner. The doll has not returned to the woman it terrorized for all those years, so it is assumed that it is happy in its new home and with its new owner.

* * *

Due to the explosion of interest in haunted dolls and other objects on eBay, an article entitled "A Guide to Buying Haunted Objects" has been posted on the site to *"raise a series of issues that each bidder should seriously consider before bidding on any haunted or enchanted item."*

The article is thoughtful and worth reading. Here is one other consideration:

If ever the phrase *caveat emptor* ("let the buyer beware") was applicable, it is in the commerce of haunted dolls. Whether you're a lonely shut-in looking for a companion, a paranormal junkie hoping for a discovery, or a bored Web surfer looking for a thrill, just remember that the cost you end up paying may be much higher than what the price tag shows.

Final Thoughts

This ends our look at some of the world's most haunted dolls. While not all are deserving of the descriptor *demonic*, as alluded to by the book's title, they all are troubling in some sense, and many most definitely deserve the moniker *truly terrible*. What makes them this way is still debatable, and will be for a very long time. There are as many theories to explain their antics as there are dolls themselves.

But the purpose of this book isn't to answer unsolvable mysteries; it is to bring awareness that such phenomena exist. Someday you may even encounter something like it yourself. According to John Zaffis, "Everyone sooner or later comes into contact with an item that puts them off or makes them feel uneasy." If this happens to you, trust your gut instinct and be watchful and aware. Things can escalate quickly when dealing with spirits. To ignore the signs could be a terrible mistake.

"My name is Talky Tina and I don't think I like you."

"My name is Talky Tina and I'm beginning to hate you."

"My name is Talky Tina, and I'm going to kill you."

– **From** *The Twilight Zone*, **Episode 126: "Living Doll"**

Selected References

Amorth, Gabriele. *An Exorcist Tells His Story*. Ignatius Press, 1999.

Austin, Joanne, Mark Moran, and Mark Sceurman. *Weird Hauntings: True Tales of Ghostly Places*. Fall River Press, 2006.

Balzano, Christopher, and Tim Weisberg. *Haunted Objects: Stories of Ghosts on Your Shelf*. Krause Publications, 2012.

Brittle, Gerald. *The Demonologist: The Extraordinary Career of Ed and Lorraine Warren*. Prentice-Hall, 1980.

Christensen, Jo-Anne. *Ghost Stories of British Columbia*. Hounslow Press, 1996.

Cliff, Martha. "Mother Spends Thousands on Toys She Claims are Haunted." *UK Daily Mail*, February 18, 2015.

Driscoll, Mike. *Demons, Deliverance, and Discernment: Separating Fact from Fiction About the Spirit World*. Catholic Answers Press, 2015.

Gotski, Charles G. "The Haunting of Matilda." *Paranormal Underground*, November 2013.

Graham, Stacey. *Haunted Stuff: Demonic Dolls, Screaming Skulls and Other Creepy Collectibles*. Llewellyn Publications, 2014.

Granato, Sherri. *Haunted America & Other Paranormal Travels*. LifeRichPublishing, 2015.

Gutelius, Scott, and Marshall Stone. *True Secrets of Key West Revealed!* Eden Entertainment, 2012.

Hutchcraft, Jak. "These People Spend Thousands of Dollars Buying 'Haunted Dolls' from eBay." *Vice.com*, March 10, 2015.

Rule, Leslie. *Ghosts Among Us: True Stories of Spirit Encounters*. Andrews McMeel Publishing, 2011.

Ryan, Joal. "How the Real Doll Behind 'Annabelle' Became Even Freakier for the Movies." *Yahoo! Movies*, October 3, 2014.

Sloan, David L. *Robert the Doll*. Phantom Press, 2014.

Zaffis, John, and Rosemary Guiley. *Haunted by the Things You Love*. Visionary Living, 2014.

Websites

Robert the Doll's Facebook Page
www.facebook.com/robert.thedoll.5

Fort East Martello Museum
www.kwahs.org

The Warren's Occult Museum
http://www.warrens.net/

The Quesnel Museum, BC
www.quesnelmuseum.ca

HD Paranormal *(formerly Haunted-Dolls.com)*
http://www.hdparanormal.com

Harold the Haunted Doll
haroldthehaunteddoll.com

The Island of the Dolls
www.isladelasmunecas.com

John Zaffis Paranormal Museum
www.johnzaffis.com

About the Author

John Harker is a freelance journalist and ghostwriter who's been writing and publishing since the 1990s. His personal encounters with unexplainable phenomena have inspired him to explore strange, dark, and disturbing topics in both non-fiction and fiction. He lives with his family in eastern Washington, where the ghosts are dry and dusty.

Also by John Harker

Ouija Board Nightmares: Terrifying True Tales

Ouija Board Nightmares 2: More True Tales of Terror

Evil Unleashed: True Tales of Spells Gone to Hell and Other Occult Disasters

A Small Request

If you have a few minutes, please consider leaving a brief review of this book. Your input is appreciated by the author and by those stopping by to browse. Thank you!

Printed in Great Britain
by Amazon